Psychopharmacology

STRAIGHT TALK ON MENTAL HEALTH MEDICATIONS

Joseph Wegmann, R.Ph., L.C.S.W

2008
Eau Claire, Wisconsin

PESI, LLC
PO Box 1000
3839 White Avenue
Eau Claire, Wisconsin 54702

Printed in the United States of America

ISBN: 9780982039816

For information on this and other PESI manuals and
audio recordings, please call 800-844-8260 or
visit our website at www.pesi.com

The field of psychopharmacology is rapidly changing. The seemingly endless introduction of new medications and even classes of medications underlines the need for a simple yet comprehensive text on the use of these psychotropic agents. This book will help the health care practitioner understand the pharmacologic basis of these drugs' actions and allow them to better understand why drug works in a specific condition.

Eugene A. Woltering MD FACS
The James D. Rives Professor of Surgery and Neurosciences
Louisiana State University Health Sciences Center
New Orleans LA

Psychopharmacology: Straight Talk on Mental Health Medications provides valuable information for nursing assessments and nurse-based patient teaching. The clear and concise method in which the information is delivered makes incorporating the facts into the nursing process an easy task.

Debra C. Godsey, RN, CLNC
Director of Nursing

Joseph Wegmann has provided training to our Child Protection staff for several years on adult as well as child/adolescent psychopharmacology. This training has been invaluable in our work with clients, understanding the use of medication in treatment of mental disorders and hopefully improving outcomes for out client population. His book will now provide our staff with a readily available and thorough manual to reference when planning our interventions with the parents and children we serve.

Robert H. Couvillon, LCSW, BACS
Regional Administrator
Covington Region Office of Community Services

THE AUTHOR:

WHO IS HE AND WHAT DOES HE DO?

Joseph Wegmann, R.Ph., LCSW is a licensed clinical pharmacist and a clinical social worker with more than thirty years of experience in the field of psychopharmacology. His diverse professional background in psychopharmacology and counseling affords him a unique perspective on medication management issues. He has consulted with numerous psychiatric facilities in the greater New Orleans, Louisiana area, and has taught psychopharmacology seminars to several thousand clinicians in 45 states.

From 1994–1997, Joe served as Clinical Director of Pharmacy Services at Touro Infirmary Hospital in New Orleans and Regional Director of Hospital Services for Premier Healthcare Corporation. He has served as Adjunct Professor of Psychopharmacology in the graduate School of Social Work at Southern University of New Orleans for 16 years, and maintains an active psychotherapy practice specializing in the treatment of depression and anxiety.

TABLE OF CONTENTS

INTRODUCTION:

THE BIGGER PICTURE —AND WHAT'S INSIDE

With medication management playing an increasingly pivotal role in the treatment of mental health disorders, the challenges faced by clinicians are increasing. For one, non-medical clinicians are the majority providers of mental health services in the United States. For another, the majority of prescriptions and orders for psychotropic medications are written not by psychiatrists, but by family practice and primary care physicians. As a result, you may be working with patients who are neither in a program of monitored drug use nor being treated with a combination of medication and psychotherapy.

Under these conditions, it is essential for all healthcare professionals—particularly those providing mental health services—to have a working knowledge of psychotropic medications. Ideally, medication prescribers and non-prescribers alike will work together to implement treatment strategies and improve clinical outcomes.

This book is organized in a straightforward, user-friendly format. It first provides a summary of disorders you might encounter, including psychoses, depression, bipolar and anxiety. This is followed by a discussion of the medication management of these disorders. The book also examines pharmacotherapy in special population groups, such as children and adolescents, pregnant women and geriatric patients.

Specific topics are also discussed, including treatment-resistant depression, the issues linked to noncompliance, and what you as a practitioner can do to address noncompliance.

With many patients self-medicating with herbal remedies, dietary supplements and vitamins, the book also outlines the herbals that have been proven beneficial in treatment—and those that pose potentially harmful interactions with prescription drugs. Finally, this book take a look at the future of psychopharmacology: Where do we go from here?

It is my hope that this unique and practical book will assist you in gaining a comprehensive understanding of the mechanisms of action, clinical applications, common adverse effects and risks of the medications most frequently prescribed in the contemporary treatment of psychiatric disorders. In practical and clinically relevant language, the goal of this book is to guide you through the maze of mental health medications, then help you identify ways to use your expanded knowledge to improve client outcomes.

Joseph Wegmann, R.Ph., L.C.S.W.
New Orleans, Louisiana

1

GETTING STARTED

THE HISTORY OF BIOLOGICAL PSYCHIATRY

Biological psychiatry is a branch of psychiatry that focuses on understanding mental disorders from a biological standpoint. More specifically, it focuses on the functions of the human nervous system.

The practice of biological psychiatry—also known as biopsychiatry—dates back to ancient times, yet the term itself was not used until the mid-20th century. That's when the research, creation and use of newly developed drugs intensified, resulting in new classes of pharmacological agents that addressed mental-health disorders, including tranquilizers, antidepressants and anti-psychotics.

DSM—BASIC PRINCIPLES OF DIAGNOSIS AND TREATMENT

Around the same time that these new drugs were emerging, the need became clear for a dependable body of knowledge that would assist clinicians in defining the approximately 100 diagnostic mental health categories used at the time. In 1952, the first *Diagnostic and Statistical Manual of Mental Health Disorders* was published. Better known by its initials "DSM," the guide is now in its fourth edition, the DSM-IV TR.

With the arrival of the DSM, the emphasis shifted away from the psychoanalytically based models and treatments of Freud, Adler and Jung—theorists and clinicians who were more interested in the *why* of a disorder than its *what*—to more descriptive and biological models and treatments. Also, where the older psychoanalytic models tended to classify *individuals*, the DSM classifies *disorders.* (Gitlin, 1996).

Today, the DSM is in effect, our mental health bible. We use the DSM to compare the signs and symptoms of our client presentations through a set of objective criteria. The DSM provides a useful guide to clinical practice by helping the clinician define disorders consistently. This, in turn, allows for a better prediction of prognosis and treatment response. (Gitlin, 1996).

The DSM employs what is known as a multi-axial approach to diagnosis. More specifically, it defines five axes:

Axis I: symptom-based clinical syndromes

Axis II: personality disorders and mental-retardation classifications

Axis III: general medical conditions

Axis IV: psychosocial stressors

Axis V: global assessment of functioning

MEDICAL MODEL

Since the age of Hippocrates, medication has been used to manage both physical and mental-health pathologies. The primary goal of the medical model is to identify these pathologies and then attempt to fix them. This is as true today as it was 2,500 years ago.

And, over time, three goals of pharmacotherapy have emerged: 1) to treat an acute disorder; 2) to prevent relapse after clinical improvement; and 3) to prevent future episodes of the disorder (Gitlin, 1996). More simply described, these are the acute, continuation and maintenance goals of medication management:

Acute treatment is initiated to ameliorate the symptoms of an actively occurring disorder. During this phase, the primary goal is to stabilize the patient using medication. Acute treatment begins with the initial prescribing of medication, and generally lasts for a period of up to six months of prescribed use, according to the National Institute of Mental Health (NIMH).

Continuation treatment is utilized to prevent relapse after the initial improvement. Here, the goal is to minimize the possibility of patient decompensation after stabilization. This period of medication use extends from six months to one year, as defined by the NIMH.

Maintenance treatment is utilized to prevent future episodes of a disorder. Two acceptable examples of this pharmacotherapy goal are the use of mood stabilizers for bipolar disorder and antipsychotics for schizophrenia. While the NIMH defines this phase as prescribed drug use for a period of one to two years, several disorders discussed in this book are linked to long term, and even lifetime prevalence of psychotropic medication utilization.

BIOLOGY OF PSYCHOPHARMACOLOGY

Pharmacokinetics, or the study of what the body does to a drug, is associated with four basic processes: absorption, distribution, metabolism and excretion.

Absorption is the movement of a substance into the bloodstream. In other words, this is the process of a substance entering the body.

Distribution involves the scattering of drugs or substances throughout body tissues and fluids.

Metabolism is the transformation or breakdown of substances such that they are prepared for elimination from the body. Metabolism occurs primarily in the liver.

Excretion is the process by which substances leave the body. Excretion occurs primarily through the kidneys.

PHARMACODYNAMICS

Pharmacodynamics is the science of drug action. Basically, it studies what a drug does to the body. More specifically, pharmacodynamics studies the mechanism of a drug action and the relationship between drug concentration and effect.

The effects that any drugs have on the body may be intended or unintended. In a "perfect drug" scenario, medications would zero in on only their intended target systems, generate only desired effects, then metabolize and leave the body. But as almost everyone who has even taken medications knows, drugs have unintended and undesirable effects as well. In this sense, they take a shotgun approach rather than a rifle approach to the body in that hopefully we get what we want from them, but at the same time unfortunately get some of what we don't want as well. For all of us, the most desired effect of any medication is its pharmacological effect, namely, does the drug actually *do* what it claims to do. Undesirable consequences of medication use include side effects, allergic reactions, rare yet potentially serious unpredictable events such as anaphylaxis and the effects on the body if a drug is abruptly discontinued.

Later on in this book, recommendations for the dosing and scheduling of medications in special population groups such as expectant mothers, children, adolescents and older adults will also be discussed. And yet another challenge facing prescribers in the future will be how to appropriately address the way that different ethnic groups respond to medication. There is evidence suggesting that several psychotropic medication classes are metabolized differently, thereby producing different response rates when prescribed to African Americans and Asians, for example. This suggests that accepted dosing practices may require modification when prescribed to those in different ethnic groups.

NEUROTRANSMITTERS

Neurotransmitters are chemicals associated with a complex series of nerve pathways that regulate what we humans think, feel and do. Medical experts have identified as many as 50 peptide neurotransmitters that have been shown to exert their effects on nerve cell function. There are probably many more as yet undiscovered, since the brain contains approximately 100 billion neurons, or nerve cells, that are regulated by these neurotransmitters.

The six neurotransmitters that are most important to psychopharmacology are: norepinephrine, serotonin, dopamine, gamma aminobutyric acid (GABA), acetylcholine and glutamate.

Norepinephrine (noradrenalin) is a hormone secreted by the adrenal glands in response to stress or arousal. It is the principal neurotransmitter of sympathetic nerve endings supplying the major organs and skin. Norepinephrine regulates alertness, anxiety, tension and the ability to have positive feelings. It is also linked to the mobilization of the body's resources during the activation of the "fight or flight" response. As such, it is released in response to an imminent danger or threat, resulting in an increase in heart rate, blood pressure and respiration. Elevated levels of norepinephrine can lead to states of increased anxiety and, in some cases, mania. Low levels of norepinephrine are implicated in depression.

Serotonin is a vasoconstrictor present in blood serum that is linked to the regulation of mood, anger, aggression, anxiety, appetite, learning, sleep, sexual functioning, states of consciousness and pain. Low levels of brain serotonin are associated with clinical depression, obsessive-compulsive disorder and anxiety disorders. Selective serotonin reuptake inhibitors (SSRIs), a class of antidepressants specific to serotonin regulation, will be discussed in Chapter 5.

Dopamine influences emotional behavior and cognition, and it regulates motor and endocrine activity, among other factors. It has numerous important roles in brain function, including attention, mood, sociability, motivation, desire, pleasure and learning. Dopamine is also strongly associated with reward mechanisms in the brain. Unusually high dopamine action can lead to psychoses and schizophrenia; many antipsychotic medications are formulated to block excess dopamine activity. Deficits in dopamine activity are implicated in attention-deficit hyperactivity disorder (ADHD). A discussion of this and the psychotic spectrum disorders will be addressed in Chapters 2, 3 and 12.

Gamma amino-butyric acid (GABA) is an amino acid that is the central nervous system's major inhibitory neurotransmitter. GABA regulation is associated with emotional balance, sleep patterns and anxiety. Low GABA levels in the limbic system—the "emotional brain"—are associated with increased anxiety, irritability and agitation. GABA activation results in decreased anxiety. This process can be facilitated through the use of benzodiazepine anti-anxiety agents, including Ativan (lorazepam), Xanax (alprazolam) and Valium (diazepam), as well as through the use of mood-stabilizing neuromodulators such as Tegretol (carbamazepine) and Depakote (divalproex). All of these drugs act to calm overall brain excitation.

Acetylcholine was the first neurotransmitter to be identified; it was discovered in the early 1900s. This neurotransmitter is released through the stimulation of the vagus nerve, which alters heart-muscle contractility. Acetylcholine is also important to functional memory, and it has been the subject of much of the research investigating cognitive dysfunction and memory deficits linked to Alzheimer's disease and other organic brain syndromes. The inhibitory or "blocking" actions of certain antidepressants on acetylcholine will be addressed in Chapter 5.

Glutamate is the brain's primary excitatory neurotransmitter. It is a basic building block of proteins and plays an important role in learning and memory. Altered glutamate functioning in schizophrenia will be discussed in Chapter 2.

2

SCHIZOPHRENIA AND ITS FIRST COUSINS

In *Surviving Schizophrenia,* E. Fuller Torrey, M.D., recounts a conversation in which he told a woman that her daughter had schizophrenia. "Anything but that!" the woman replied in horror. "Why couldn't she have leukemia or some other disease?"

Dr. Torrey reassured the mother that schizophrenia was much more treatable than a cancer that might cost the girl her life. Yet the woman answered sadly, "I would still prefer that my daughter had leukemia."

Such is the stigma that this psychiatric disorder carries, made worse by the way our society treats those afflicted with it. According to the National Institute of Mental Health (NIMH), approximately 2.2 million Americans are diagnosed with schizophrenia at any given time, with almost a million of those failing to receive adequate treatment. An alarming number of homeless people suffer from schizophrenia—perhaps as high as 40 percent, say some statistics—and are likely to be rotated among the streets, shelters, emergency rooms, public psychiatric assistance programs and even the jails.

To be sure, those suffering from schizophrenia can be disturbing. They hear voices, experience hallucinations, speak incoherently, break out in senseless laughter, weep and rage without provocation, or are catatonic. Prior to 1954, when Thorazine (chlorpromazine) was approved in the United States for psychiatric treatment, these individuals were certainly feared. Because society couldn't make sense of schizophrenics' behavior, they were routinely confined to asylums. Little was known about their effective treatment or rehabilitation.

But today, as more has been learned about the brain, nutrition, genetics, environmental factors and of course, new medications and other therapies, the outlook for treating schizophrenia has improved markedly. While the DSM-IV TR no longer uses the terms primary and secondary psychoses, for diagnostic purposes clinicians still use certain criteria to determine which types of psychotic disorders are being presented. More specifically, when the only pathology is the psychotic disorder itself, it is known as a primary psychosis. When the symptoms are a result of a general medical condition or are substance-induced, it is known as secondary psychosis. Also, a distinction is made between psychosis and schizophrenia. Psychosis is a general term that describes psychotic features; schizophrenia is a type of psychosis.

MAJOR PSYCHOTIC SPECTRUM DISORDERS

Brief psychotic disorder. This is a psychosis that has a rapid onset and generally follows an identifiable stressor. It is characterized by emotional turmoil, mood changes and confusion, along with the presence of one or more schizophrenic symptoms. Brief psychotic disorder is time-limited, lasting at least one day but no more than one month.

Delusional disorder. This involves the creation of sometimes elaborate, non-bizarre delusions—something that could be true, but likely isn't. For example, the person believes that their husband or wife is having an affair, when in fact the person is faithful. The delusion consumes the lives of these individuals as they become utterly convinced that what they believe is actually happening, despite evidence to the contrary.

Schizoaffective disorder. With this condition, a person exhibits features of both schizophrenia—such as delusions, hallucinations and thought distortion—and a mood component, such as depression or mania. The diagnosis is made when the person has features of both illnesses, but does not strictly meet criteria for either schizophrenia or a mood disorder alone. For this reason, achieving diagnostic accuracy is quite difficult.

Schizophreniform disorder. This is often referred to as a "short episode of schizophrenia." Symptoms are similar to those of schizophrenia; they last longer than one month, but less than six months. Roughly half of all those diagnosed with schizopheniform disorder are subsequently diagnosed with schizophrenia.

Schizophrenia. The "granddaddy" of the psychotic spectrum disorders, schizophrenia involves a psychotic phase characterized by prominent psychotic features, such as delusions, hallucinations and gross impairment in reality testing. By definition, this psychotic phase must last for at least one month. Schizophrenia also causes social, occupational and other vocational functional impairment that must last for at least six months.

Evidence suggests that schizophrenia has a significant genetic component. Its onset is also considerably influenced by psychosocial, and environmental factors, as well as by stressors. This cruel and chronically debilitating disorder affects approximately 1 percent of the U.S. population and is a leading cause of disability.

Schizophrenia affects men and women differently. For men, the adult onset age is typically 18 to 20, while for women, it is typically in the mid-twenties. Adolescent age onset typically occurs between the ages of 11 to 15 for both boys and girls. Childhood-onset schizophrenia is considered rare, with a rate of probability less than 1 in 10,000. Because it is so rare, a detailed history is essential to confirm diagnostic accuracy.

Etiology

From a neurophysiological perspective, several neurotransmitters—most notably dopamine and glutamate—have been implicated in the development of schizophrenia. The hyperactivity of dopamine in the limbic system pathway is a consistent finding. The hypofunction of glutamate could also be responsible for certain aspects of schizophrenia.

Diagnosing schizophrenia or any of its associated subtypes is difficult for several reasons: The disorder is complex, symptoms may appear only briefly, and symptoms may be present in conjunction with other disorders.

Figure 2-1. Subtypes of Schizophrenia

Paranoid:	The most common type of schizophrenia. Symptoms include either continuous or intermittent hallucinations and delusions that involve perceived ridicule, threats or commands; or the feeling of being followed or chosen for a special mission.
Disorganized:	Tends toward verbal incoherence and strange behaviors. Patients can engage in long, nonsensical conversation, express aggravation, or laugh inappropriately.
Catatonic:	Characterized by emotional withdrawal and social isolation.
Residual:	Usually lasts for one year and occurs after the disappearance of positive symptoms and emergence of negative symptoms. There is apathy and loss of interest in social contact.
Undifferentiated:	Symptoms of schizophrenia are exhibited but do not fit into a particular category.

SYMPTOM DOMAINS OF SCHIZOPHRENIA

Positive symptoms are not positive in the ordinary sense of the word. They are described as such because they are the active, observable and treatable symptoms of the disorder. These include both delusions—false fixed beliefs held with conviction—and hallucinations, including auditory, visual and other false and abnormal perceptions.

Negative symptoms are those that "negate" or take away from the schizophrenic's core personality. These include:

- Blunted affect, which can manifest as a type of "masked," expressionless look
- Emotional withdrawal
- Passivity and apathy
- Anhedonia, or the inability to experience pleasure

Cognitive Symptoms. Examples of neurocognitive deficits include:

- Impaired executive function: poor problem-solving, reduced capacity to accommodate and assimilate new information

- Attention deficits
- Impaired memory function
- Impaired informational processing

In addition, schizophrenics can become combative, sometimes in conjunction with fear, as a result of hallucinations and delusional or confusing thoughts. This aggression can manifest itself in both verbal and physical attacks, acting out sexually, self-mutilation and suicide attempts. About half of all schizophrenics attempt suicide as a result of "command" delusions, hallucinations or major depression, and 10 percent of them eventually succeed.

MEDICAL DISORDERS INFLUENCING PSYCHOTIC FEATURES

Medical disorders that can influence psychotic manifestations must be ruled out in order to make an accurate diagnosis of schizophrenia. These medical disorders include:

- Infections
- Tumors
- End-stage renal disease
- Hypoglycemia
- Dementias
- Stroke
- Head injuries
- Vitamin deficiencies, particularly thiamine (vitamin B_1)

DRUGS INFLUENCING PSYCHOTIC FEATURES

- Cannabis (marijuana)
- Amphetamines
- Hallucinogens
- Alcohol
- Opiates

WHAT SCHIZOPHRENIA IS *NOT*

Schizophrenia is a complicated and multifaceted disease, and this has led to some unfortunate and ingrained stereotypes that are difficult for patients and their families to deal with. Contrary to these stereotypes, schizophrenics are not necessarily evil, dangerous, retarded, addicted or weak. Also, despite the root word meaning "split mind," schizophrenia does not imply a split personality or multiple personalities.

In spite of the many challenges, schizophrenia is treatable and manageable with a host of medications, some of which can be used in combination in order to achieve a positive patient outcome. Those will be discussed in detail in Chapter 3.

3

MEDICATING THE SPLIT MIND

The modern era for the treatment of psychotic disorders commenced in the early 1950s, when Thorazine (chlorpromazine) was found to be an effective treatment for patients with schizophrenia. Numerous other antipsychotics were then developed and released as treatments for those suffering from psychosis. Today, medication management remains the mainstay of treatment for the psychotic disorders

HOW ANTIPSYCHOTIC MEDICATIONS WORK

Figure 3-1

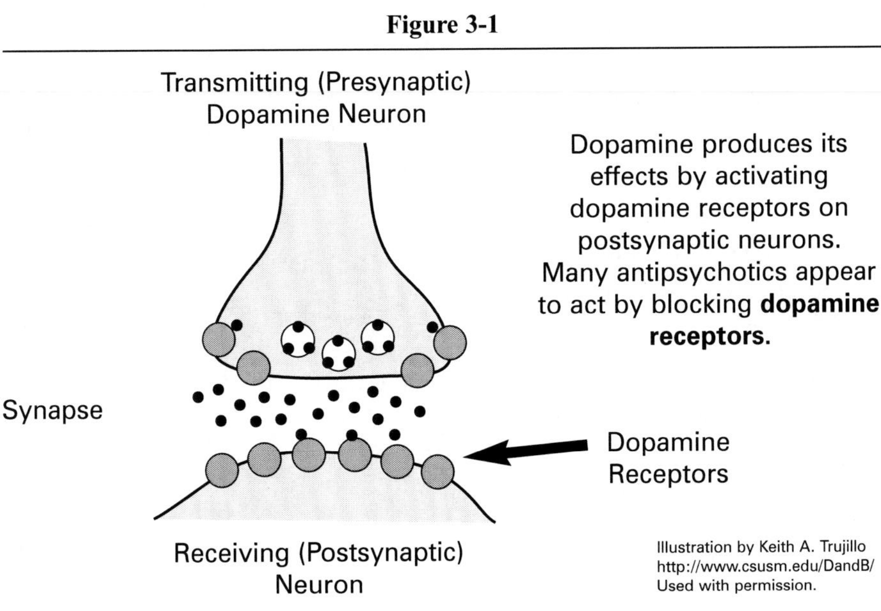

All antipsychotic medications block dopamine receptors in the central nervous system. The blocking actions on dopamine receptors in the limbic system are thought to underlie the effectiveness in managing the "positive" symptoms of schizophrenia discussed in Chapter 2. However, because of their actions on a number of neurotransmitter systems, a veritable host of side effects may emerge. These are powerful drugs, and like all medications, they have both their benefits and risks.

When these drugs are effective, the patient feels more relaxed, less fearful, more confident and better able to concentrate. Antipsychotics may or may not sedate the patient, depending on product selection. Also, thought distortion, mood and sleep patterns may improve, too.

Antipsychotic medications fall into two main categories: the older conventional agents and the newer atypical agents.

Conventional agents: The first antipsychotic to emerge on the U.S. drug market was Thorazine (chlorpromazine) in 1952. Others followed, including Haldol (haloperidol), Navane (thiothixene) and Stelazine (trifluperazine). Today, these first-generation medications are no longer considered the agents of choice for treating psychotic manifestations, having given way over the past several years to the newer atypical or second-generation antipsychotics. All of these first-generation agents are effective in treating mania but ineffective in managing bipolar depression. Conventional antipsychotics fell out of favor due to pivotal shortcomings, two in particular. First, they are responsible for a group of neurological side effects known as the extrapyramidal side effects (EPS). Second, approximately 20 percent of adult schizophrenics are unresponsive to conventional antipsychotics.

Atypical antipsychotic agents: Over the past 17 years, a new generation of agents has emerged. These so-called atypical or second-generation drugs were developed to meet the treatment needs of those unresponsive to the conventional agents and to improve the overall tolerability of antipsychotic use.

SIDE EFFECTS OF THE CONVENTIONAL AGENTS

As stated earlier, extrapyramidal symptoms (EPS) refer to a neurological side effect of antipsychotic drugs, and they are common with the use of the conventional agents. Those occurring most often include:

Dystonia: The most common manifestation of EPS, it is characterized by muscle-tightening in the neck and shoulders, accompanied by spasms.

Parkinsonism EPS: Produces muscle rigidity, mask-like facies, tremor, shuffling gait and diminished arm-swing.

Akathisia: This type of EPS is characterized by motor-restlessness, a need to move and an inability to sit still.

Tardive dyskinesia: Though not a type of EPS, it is a most feared adverse effect. It is characterized by involuntary facial movements involving the tongue, eyes, lips and face. Tardive dyskinesia is generally associated with long-term use of conventional antipsychotics. Once present, it is considered irreversible, although some patients show a slow remission of symptoms over time.

When an EPS develops, one treatment is to lower the dosage of the offending drug. But pharmacological treatments can also be utilized. Agents such as Benadryl (diphenhydramine) and Cogentin (benztropine) can be administered either orally or intramuscularly.

Other side effects of the conventional agents may include:

- Dry mouth, blurred vision, constipation, sedation and memory problems
- Orthostatic hypotension, a drop in standing blood pressure
- Weight gain, particularly with Thorazine (chlorpromazine)
- Grand mal seizures
- Increased levels of prolactin (a hormone related to growth hormone)
- Neuroleptic malignant syndrome

MORE ABOUT ATYPICAL ANTIPSYCHOTIC AGENTS

The term "atypical" helps differentiate these antipsychotics from the older, conventional ones. More important, however, is that the atypicals are not a single, homogeneous class of drugs. Instead, they differ from one another with respect to receptor affinity, effectiveness and side effects. Also, because of their blocking action on both dopamine and a serotonin receptor subtype, these agents carry a lower risk of extrapyramidal side effects and tardive dyskinesia. From a comparative standpoint, some of the atypicals are more effective than the conventional antipsychotics in reducing the negative symptoms of schizophrenia. All of the atypicals treat mania.

Currently, there are seven atypical antipsychotics available on the U.S. drug market:

> Clozaril (clozapine): Introduced in 1990, this was the first of the atypical medications and was considered a godsend by otherwise treatment-resistant patients. Clozaril is the prototype to this day, considered to be the most effective, but also the most dangerous.

Figure 3-2. A Double-Edged Sword

Clozaril (clozapine) was introduced in the United States in 1990, after being used in Europe since the 1970s. Although this drug has been extremely successful in treating schizophrenia, it also carries more than its share of risks. For this reason, it is not a first-line drug of choice, and careful monitoring is necessary.

Benefits:

- Some improvement in cognitive function
- Effective in decreasing hallucinations and delusions
- FDA-approved for the treatment of recurrent suicidal behavior
- Can help with smoking cessation in some patients
- Can diminish symptoms of aggression and violence
- Can decrease alcohol use in patients who abuse alcohol
- Very low incidence of EPS and akathisia
- Almost no tardive dyskinesia

Risks:

- May cause agranulocytosis, a potentially fatal decrease in white blood cell count that can subject a patient to opportunistic infection
- Blood work (particularly WBC counts) are mandated by the FDA according to established guidelines
- Can interact with other drugs that also decrease WBC count, such as Tegretol (carbamazepine) and some antibiotics

- Some deaths have been reported, due to myocarditis, an inflammation or degeneration of the heart muscle
- Oversedation
- Major weight gain
- Can cause urinary incontinence
- Seizures at higher doses are common
- May take many weeks, even months, to be effective

Risperdal (risperidone): This medication is well-accepted for the treatment of agitation and aggression in dementia, and in bipolar disorders. It is also effective in minimizing the temper tantrums, aggression and self-injury associated with autism, as well as disruptive behavior disorders in children and adolescents. Risperdal (risperidone) gained FDA approval in 2007 for the treatment of schizophrenia in adolescents ages 13 to 17. It is available in a long acting injection formulation named Risperdal Consta (risperidone microspheres IM).

Zyprexa (olanzapine): This drug has documented efficacy as an augmenting agent to SSRI antidepressants in nonpsychotic, treatment-resistant major depressive disorders. It was the first atypical antipsychotic approved for the treatment of acute bipolar mania, is effective in the management of bipolar depression and the maintenance treatment of bipolar disorder. It generally produces the most weight gain among the atypicals. Zyprexa (olanzapine) demonstrates more efficacy than most other atypical antipsychotics. There is no long acting formulation of the drug, but an injectable and a rapidly dissolving pill are available.

Seroquel (quetiapine): Studies support the use of this drug for the management of aggressive, cognitive and affective symptoms of schizophrenia. It is effective in the treatment of bipolar depression. There is essentially no EPS or tardive dyskinesia with this medication. It is also catching on as a treatment for insomnia, aggressive outbursts, and, most recently, traumatic nightmares associated with post-traumatic stress disorder (PTSD). The drug is typically dosed twice a day. Reviews have not shown Seroquel (quetiapine) to have increased efficacy over Haldol (haloperidol).

Geodon (ziprasidone): This is the least likely of the atypicals to cause weight gain, and it is also the least sedating. Its unique pharmacological profile suggests potential advantages for associated anxiety and depression, although the drug is associated with agitation at lower doses. But because Geodon (ziprasidone) has been linked to cases of fatal cardiac arrhythmia, it is not a first-line treatment of choice. For this reason, a thorough cardiac work-up is recommended before use. Geodon (ziprasidone) is available as an intramuscular injection.

Abilify (aripiprazole): Referred to as the "miracle drug" of the new millennium, it is becoming well established as an effective treatment for a number of disorders. Although its antipsychotic efficacy does not rival that of other second generation antipsychotics. Abilify (aripiprazole) is often employed in managing the aggressive outbursts of mentally retarded children. It is also used to treat Tourette's syndrome and as an augmenting agent to SSRIs in treatment-resistant cases of OCD. Research is robust for this medication in the prevention of relapse in bipolar disorder. Abilify (aripiprazole) is associated with minimal weight gain, and has few side effects. The drug was approved by the FDA in 2007 for the treatment of schizophrenia in adolescents ages 13 to 17.

Invega (paliperidone): Invega, released in 2007, is the most recent addition to the atypical antipsychotic group. It is actually an active metabolite of Risperdal (risperidone); note the similarity in their generic names. Because its delivery system to the bloodstream allows for extended action (24 hours), it can be dosed once daily. Reputable clinical studies indicate that Invega (paliperidone) has no clear therapeutic advantages over Risperidal (risperidone) or, for that matter, the other atypicals. Similar to Geodon (ziprasidone), it also carries some cardiac risk and is metabolized primarily by the kidneys, so it is not associated with as many potential drug interactions. Janssen, the manufacturer of Invega (paliperidone) and Risperdal (risperidone), stopped issuing Risperdal (risperidone) samples in June, 2008 due to patent expiration.

SIDE EFFECTS OF THE ATYPICAL AGENTS

In general, the side effects of the atypical agents are more benign than those of the older, conventional agents. As mentioned previously, there is less EPS and a lower risk of tardive dyskinesia. The most common side effects of the atypicals are weight gain, sedation, insomnia, agitation, constipation and dry mouth.

However, both Zyprexa (olanzapine) and Clozaril (clozapine) have been linked to an increased risk of Type II diabetes and an additional risk of increasing triglycerides and cholesterol. Geodon (ziprasidone) and Abilify (aripiprazole) carry a low risk for both diabetes and worsening triglyceride and cholesterol levels.

Effective treatment of schizophrenia continues to be elusive. Reliable, valid studies fail to demonstrate that negative symptoms and cognitive problems are responding to any of our present medications, creating a genuine dilemma for both clinicians and patients.

WHAT YOU, YOUR CLIENTS AND FAMILY MEMBERS NEED TO KNOW

Relapse in schizophrenia is common, due to noncompliance with medications. With schizophrenics, typically two things happen: First, they take their medications, start to feel better, and then stop, believing they are "cured." Second, patients in the throes of a psychotic episode can be convinced that the medications are really a poison or a form of mind control. The patient's family is often in a position to observe the prodromal symptoms—early warning signs of the symptom's possible return—so involving the family in discussions about the significant benefits of medication compliance can be important and helpful.

CASE STUDY: SCHIZOPHRENIA—"THE VOICES WERE TELLING ME"

Leonard is a 22-year-old homeless man who was recently arrested for bathing nude in a fountain adjacent to an upscale hotel. The police have transported Leonard to a private psychiatric facility at which you are a clinical social worker, and his case is referred to you. It is difficult to obtain a clear history from Leonard, because he rambles incessantly, often changing the subject while making bizarre and incoherent statements. He is able to report, however, that during the last month he has been generally unable to sleep, and that when he did sleep, he often experienced what he calls "strange dreams." Leonard appears emaciated and reeks of alcohol. When asked about his arrest, Leonard states that he simply found the hotel fountain a convenient location for a bath.

Leonard admits to hearing voices over the past few weeks, and he reports that on the day he was arrested, the voices were telling him to "be sure to bathe the feet of all the passers-by, because this was Holy Week." He explains that he was just getting ready to do that when "someone from the hotel reported me."

Because of Leonard's indigent status, your facility's case management department asks you to refer Leonard to a state-operated psychiatric hospital. After a consultation with a psychiatrist at the state facility, you are made aware that Leonard is well known to the staff. The psychiatrist mentions that Leonard is routinely treated with psychiatric medication, and that upon symptom remission, he is released. The doctor adds that numerous attempts to locate any of Leonard's family members or friends have failed, as have all attempts to locate placement for him, because "he doesn't follow the rules." The doctor concludes by saying that Leonard is one of the facility's many "revolving door" patients that they expect to see repeatedly over time.

Diagnostic Considerations

Given that Leonard is well known to the staff at the state psychiatric facility, he had previously been diagnosed with chronic paranoid schizophrenia. Leonard's psychotic symptoms improved markedly on Risperdal (risperidone) in the past, so the attending psychiatrist decided to begin with 2 mg (in divided doses) on day one of treatment. The dosing regimen was increased by 2 mg per day to a total daily dose of 8 mg over a four-day course of administration.

Treatment Course

Leonard remained in the hospital for another three days and then was discharged on 8 mg of Risperdal (risperidone) per day after demonstrating much symptom improvement. Leonard's prognosis for maintaining symptom remission was poor, however, given his tendencies toward medication non-compliance after getting better and his decision to remain homeless.

DOSAGE RANGE CHART — ANTIPSYCHOTIC MEDICATIONS

BRAND NAME	GENERIC NAME	CLASS	DAILY DOSAGE RANGE*
Abilify	aripiprazole	atypical	10 mg - 30 mg
Clozaril	clozapine	atypical	300 mg - 600mg
Geodon	ziprasidone	atypical	120 mg -160 mg
Haldol	haloperidol	conventional	1 mg – 40 mg
Invega	paliperidone	atypical	3 mg – 12 mg
Mellaril	thioridazine	conventional	150 mg – 800 mg
Moban	molindone	conventional	20 mg - 225 mg
Navane	thiothixene	conventional	10 mg - 60 mg
Prolixin	fluphenazine	conventional	3 mg - 45 mg
Risperdal	risperidone	atypical	4 mg - 16 mg
Seroquel	quetiapine	atypical	300 mg - 600 mg
Stelazine	trifluoperazine	conventional	2 mg - 40 mg
Thorazine	chlorpromazine	conventional	60 mg - 800 mg
Zyprexa	olanzapine	atypical	5 mg - 20 mg

* Suggested adult dose

Note: Dosage ranges may vary depending on source, and may also vary according to age.

4

DEPRESSION: MORE THAN JUST FEELING THE BLUES

In the United States, depression is a major cause of disability, much like heart disease, diabetes and chronic pain. Yet according to the National Institute of Mental Health, only 30 percent of people with depression are ever diagnosed. Of this 30 percent, only half are treated. And of these, only 6 percent are sufficiently managed.

Think of the numbers this way: If you take 100 people with depression, only 30 of them will ever be diagnosed. Of these 30, only 15 will receive any form of medical therapy. And of these 15, only one person will be managed adequately at least some of the time.

The bottom line: Many depressed people—particularly those who enter the treatment system through family practice or primary care—fall through the cracks from a management perspective. This occurs for a variety of reasons, the most prevalent being a lack of both patient and physician follow-up after the initial appointment. It is crucial, therefore, for clinicians to understand the differential diagnosis of this group of clinical syndromes in order to affect positive treatment outcomes.

UNIPOLAR DEPRESSIONS

Unipolar depression, synonymous with the terms *clinical depression* and *major depressive disorder*, is a prolonged state characterized by a group of symptoms that affect thoughts, behavior and feelings, and interfere with functioning. These symptoms include persistent sadness or despair, feelings of low self-esteem, apathy, pessimistic thinking, emotional hypersensitivity, irritability, the inability to experience pleasure, and thoughts of suicide. Mental-health professionals look for a particular combination of symptoms over a significant period of time to arrive at a diagnosis of depression.

Figure 4-1. American Psychiatric Association Diagnostic Criteria for Major Depressive Episode

After ruling out symptoms that are due to a physical condition, mood-incongruent delusions or hallucinations, incoherence, or marked loosening of associations, patients must exhibit at least five of the following symptoms during the same two-week period. At least one of those symptoms is either depressed mood, or loss of interest or functioning.

- Depressed mood most of the day, nearly every day. In children and adolescents this can be irritable mood.
- Loss of interest, or diminished pleasure, in all, or almost all activities for most of the day, nearly every day.
- Changes in appetite, including weight loss or gain of more than five percent of body weight in one month. In children, this would be a failure to gain expected weight.
- Insomnia or hypersomnia (sleeping too much)
- Psychomotor agitation or retardation nearly every day, as observable by others.
- Fatigue or low energy
- Feelings of worthlessness or inappropriate guilt, not just self-reproach or guilt for being sick
- Indecisiveness or difficulty in thinking or concentrating
- Recurrent suicidal ideation with no specific plan; suicide attempt or a specific suicide plan

Adapted from: Diagnostic and Statistical Manual of Mental Disorders, 4th ed. 1994. Washington, DC: American Psychiatric Association (APA).

It is useful to think of these depressions as "typecast," so to speak. There's the reactive type, the biological type, the mixed type, and an atypical type, to name just a few manifestations.

A *reactive* depression, which the DSM–IV TR refers to as Adjustment Disorder with Depressed Mood, can range in intensity from mild or moderate to severe. The word "reactive" is an accurate depiction of what is happening in this type of depression. Reactive depressions typically occur in response to a specific external event.

Death, divorce and job loss are three examples of psychosocial stressors that could trigger a reactive depression. A "pure" reactive depression—although it is doubtful that such a thing exists—is not associated with changes in physical functioning such as sleep, energy levels and appetite.

Physical depressions—often referred to as biological depressions—on the other hand, typically emerge in the absence of precipitating psychosocial events. Instead, these depressions are endogenous in nature; that is, they "come from within." Biological depressions are associated with physiological changes in the body's system. They often present with one or more of these core symptoms: a change in appetite, change in sleep patterns, psychomotor retardation (thought slowdown accompanied by a decrease in physical movements), anhedonia (the inability to experience pleasure) and decreased libido.

Physical depressions can be medically based. It is hypothesized that certain medical conditions may interfere with neurotransmission in the brain, possibly inhibiting the central nervous system's capacity to get sufficient amounts of the nerve chemicals—norepinephrine, serotonin and dopamine, for example—in the right place and at appropriate levels. Diabetes and hypothyroidism are two common culprits influencing depression, with the latter implicated in as many as 10 percent of all severe depressions. In these cases, a thyroid function panel that includes a measure of TSH (thyroid stimulating hormone) is recommended. Hormonal events can also trigger a biological depression. In women, changes in progestin, estrogen and testosterone levels around the menses can lead to agitation, irritability, insomnia and the possible development of Premenstrual Dysphoric Disorder (PMDD). Low testosterone levels in aging men can cause depression. It is estimated that 20 percent of men between the ages of 60 and 80 have low testosterone levels. Additionally, prescription and recreational drug use or neurochemical imbalances in the brain can cause chemical changes resulting in a biological-type depression.

Table 4-1. Medical, Drug and Hormonal Influences on Depression	
Medical Conditions:	• Autoimmune disorders: AIDS, rheumatoid arthritis, systemic lupus erythematosus, etc. • Neurological disorders:Parkinson's disease, etc.
Substance Induced:	• Prescription medications and recreational drugs (Table 4-2).
Hormonal Irregularities:	• In women: menopause, premenstrual, postpartum. • In men: low testosterone in mid- to late life.

Mixed depression is a type of depression involving both reactive and biological features. It is a result of brain function that appears to succumb to the effects of psychological stress. When events are extremely stressful, biological changes can occur in the brain, leading to this type of depression.

Neither truly exogenous nor endogenous, mixed depressions most likely represent the majority of depressions seen clinically. Typical onset is consistent with the more classic reactive depressions outlined above. But physiological symptoms can develop over time, particularly if the patient does not respond to psychotherapy.

Atypical depression is the most common form of depression, accounting for perhaps 40 percent of the total depressed population. This form is best thought of as a more severe manifestation of biological depression. The presence of co-existing anxiety disorders seems to be the rule; patients are likely to experience such syndromes as panic disorder and social phobias. In addition, the atypical depressive tends to eat and sleep too much, feel irritable and agitated, and become significantly hypersensitive to rejection.

DYSTHYMIA

Dysthymia—from the Greek root meaning "bad mind"—is a chronic, low-grade "functional" depression characterized by depressive symptoms that last a minimum of two years in adults and one year in children and adolescents. Symptoms are not absent for more than two months, and they are not caused by a medical condition or drugs. Dysthymics tend to be a uniformly unhappy lot of individuals, yet most of them do not seek treatment. The symptoms are similar to those of major depressive episodes, only milder.

The long-term prevalence of symptom presentation tends to take an exacting toll on the productivity and overall quality of life of people with dysthymia. They are also at high risk for escalation. As many as 80 percent of dysthymics experience at least one episode of a major depressive disorder. These more severe episodes, in turn, mask the underlying chronic dysthymic depression. The result is a "double depression."

Figure 4-2. American Psychiatric Association Diagnostic Criteria for Dysthymia

- Depressed mood for most of the day, nearly every day, for at least two years. In children and adolescents, this can be irritable mood for at least one year.
- In this depressed mood, the patient experiences at least two of the following, and has not been free of these symptoms during the two-year time period (one year for children and adolescents):

  - Changes in appetite – eating too much or too little
  - Insomnia or hypersomnia (sleeping too much)
  - Fatigue, loss of energy
  - Poor self-esteem
  - Indecisiveness, difficulty in thinking or concentrating
  - Feelings of hopelessness

- Symptoms are not present only in conjunction with another chronic disorder, and are not caused by a medical condition.
- Symptoms are not caused by substance abuse (alcohol, drugs, medications).
- Symptoms interfere with functioning at work, home, and other areas, and are a source of great distress.
- No manic, mixed, or hypomanic episode
- No major depressive episode during the two-year time period (one year for children and adolescents)

Adapted from: Diagnostic and Statistical Manual of Mental Disorders, 4th ed. 1994. Washington, DC: American Psychiatric Association (APA).

THE ROLE DRUGS PLAY IN INFLUENCING DEPRESSION

Alcohol or any other central nervous system depressant—such as the benzodiazepines, opiates and barbiturates—can worsen depression. Through the chronic use of alcohol, the brain's pleasure center floods with the chemical dopamine. But there comes a point where the brain's mechanism of homeostasis attempts to restore the balance. This can trigger a drop in concentrations of dopamine, often leading to depression.

A similar thing can happen to those chronically using benzodiazepines, such as Valium (diazepam), Ativan (lorazepam) and Xanax (alprazolam), for daytime anxiety and insomnia. Benzodiazepines such as these, particularly if used excessively and at doses that exceed the recommended daily maximums, can enhance the actions of GABA only so much before some patients report feeling more anxious or experiencing more insomnia problems than they did before they started taking the drug.

Anti-hypertensives (medications used to treat high blood pressure), anti-Parkinson's agents and beta-blockers have also been linked to a dysfunctional synthesis of norepinephrine, serotonin and dopamine.

Corticosteroids (including cortisone and prednisone), which some patients take for such autoimmune disorders as systemic lupus and multiple sclerosis, can be problematic, too. These can cause not only depression, but even psychotic features. These episodes emerge primarily through high-dose, long-term use.

Table 4-2 Prescription and Recreational Drugs that Can Cause Depression

Brand	**Generic**	**Type**
Catapres	clonidine	antihypertensive
Cortone	cortisone acetate	corticosteroid
DepoProvera	medroxyprogesterone	progestin
Dopar	levodopa	anti-parkinsons
Estrace	estradiol	estrogen
Estraderm	estradiol	estrogen
Flagyl	metronidazole	antibiotic; antiparasitic
Inderal	propranolol	beta-blocker
Larodopa	levodopa	anti-parkinsons
Librium	chlordiazepoxide	benzodiazepine
Ogen	estropipate	estrogen
Premarin	conjugated equine estrogens	estrogen
Provera	medroxyprogesterone	progestin
Reglan	metoclopramide	anti-emetic (anti-nausea)
Sinemet	levodopa/carbidopa	anti-parkinsons
Symmetrel	amantadine	anti-parkinsons
Valium	diazepam	benzodiazepine
Xanax	alprazolam	benzodiazepine

Recreational drugs:
alcohol
amphetamines
opiates
cocaine
marijuana

5

ANTIDEPRESSANTS: WHAT THEY ARE AND HOW THEY WORK

In 1990, Prozac became the first drug to be featured on the cover of a major U.S. news magazine, marking a turning point in pharmaceutical history. Prozac (fluoxetine), hailed as a "miracle" drug of sorts, was introduced in the United States in 1988. Two years later it was the most widely prescribed drug in this country, earning a place as *Newsweek*'s "cover drug" with the headline "Prozac: A Breakthrough Drug for Depression."

Prozac may have emerged as a 20th century star, but many antidepressants have long been effective in managing not only unipolar depression, but also bipolar disorder, obsessive compulsive disorder, social anxiety disorder, substance abuse, panic disorder, eating disorders, premenstrual disorders and anxiety disorders.

Fortunately for its more than 18 million sufferers, clinical depression is one of the most treatable of psychiatric illnesses. Medication, psychotherapy or a combination of the two is successful in more than 80 percent of cases.

HOW ANTIDEPRESSANTS WORK

A primary role of medication is to restore normal biological functioning. For antidepressants, the location of that functioning resides in the 100 billion nerve cells that are contained within the human brain. The nervous system depends on communication among these many nerve cells.

THE STRUCTURE

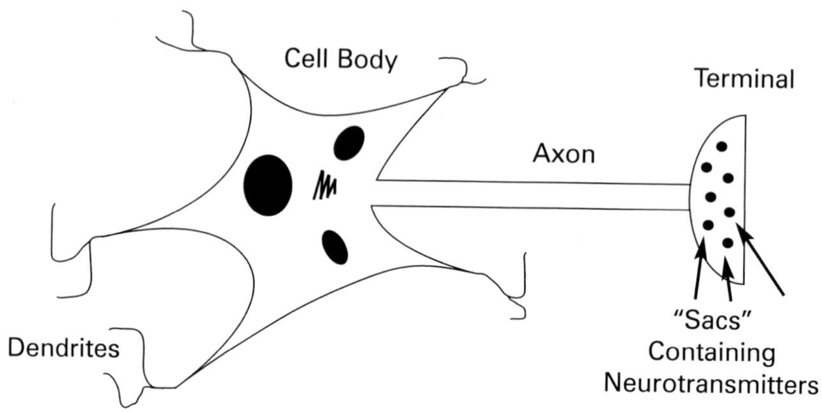

A nerve cell consists of a cell body, dendrites, an axon and a terminal.

Each *cell body* manufactures its own messenger molecules, more typically referred to as neurotransmitters. For the sake of this discussion, these are norepinephrine, serotonin, dopamine and GABA.

Dendrites are structures, shaped like tree branches, that fan out from the cell body. They accept and send information to the cell body, serving as a message-exchange system that facilitates intracellular communication.

Axons are fibrous tubes that serve to transmit impulses away from the cell body. After the neurotransmitters are manufactured, they travel along this tube-like passageway away from the body of the cell. Then they are stored within small "sacs" or vesicles within the presynaptic *terminal*.

THE PROCESS

From the terminal, the intercellular communication process causes the release of neurotransmitters into a *synapse*, a tiny gap between nerve cells. The nerve cell that releases the neurochemicals into the synapse is called the *presynaptic* neuron. The nerve cell that receives the neurochemicals is called the *postsynaptic* neuron.

Once the neurotransmitter molecules are released by the presynaptic cell, they migrate across the synapse through a series of chemical and electrical impulses. They are then capable of binding to *receptors* that are located on the surface of the postsynaptic nerve cell.

Receptors are tiny proteins that serve as catcher's mitts, intercepting neurotransmitter molecules as they whiz by. These are specific catcher's mitts—norepinephrine attaches only to a norepinephrine receptor; serotonin attaches only to a serotonin receptor, and so on. The binding of neurotransmitters to receptors, like a key fitting into a lock, essentially facilitates this intercellular communication, namely the way one nerve cell impacts the functioning of or "talks" to another nerve cell. For this reason, neurotransmitters are referred to as "primary messengers."

Some of the neurotransmitters released into the synapse bind to postsynaptic receptors. Others are chemically degraded by enzymes, such as monoamine oxidase. Still others are rapidly reabsorbed back into presynaptic cells. This re-absorption occurs by way of a *reuptake transporter pump*. This pump facilitates a recycling process that allows neurotransmitters to be repackaged and reused.

Many antidepressants operate by way of reuptake inhibition, in which the drug molecule blocks the pores of the reuptake transporter pump. This lets neurotransmitters released into the synaptic cleft stay for a longer period of time, thus potentially enhancing postsynaptic nerve cell actions.

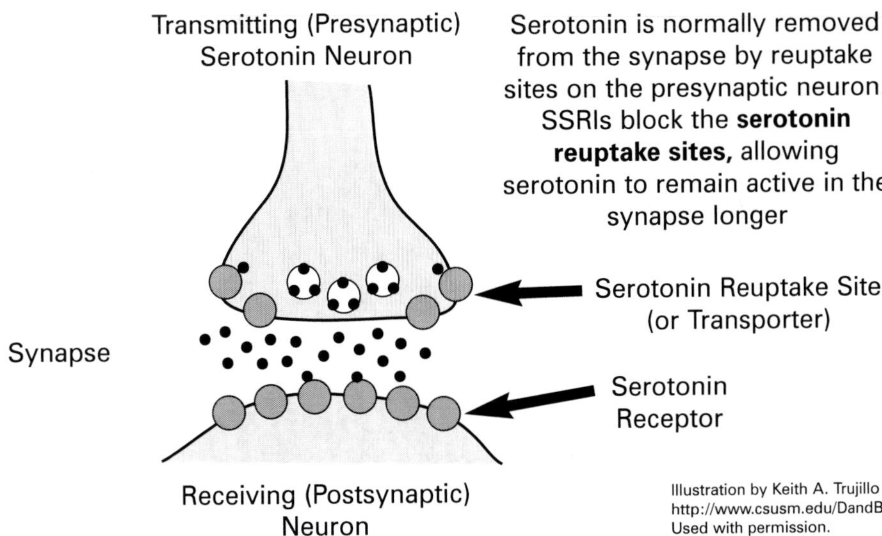

Illustration by Keith A. Trujillo
http://www.csusm.edu/DandB/
Used with permission.

ANTIDEPRESSANTS

All of the antidepressants have similar efficacy, and most of them have different side effects. At least 50 percent of clients who will respond to antidepressants begin to demonstrate improvement in the first few days to a week. Remission of depression, however, is much more difficult to achieve and may take eight to twelve weeks.

The U.S. drug market now offers six major categories of antidepressants:

- Cyclics
- Selective serotonin reuptake inhibitors (SSRIs)
- Serotonin and norepinephrine reuptake inhibitors (SNRIs)
- Norepinephrine reuptake inhibitors (NRIs)
- Monoamine oxidase inhibitors (MAOIs)
- Atypical antidepressants

CYCLICS

Also referred to as tricyclics, these are among the oldest group of antidepressants, dating from the 1950s. One of the very first cyclics, Tofranil (imipramine), was originally developed as an antispychotic, but was subsequently found to possess antidepressant properties. Other cyclics include Elavil (amitriptyline), Anafranil (clomipramine) and Desyrel (trazodone). Many of these agents are dual-action in that they block the reuptake of both serotonin and norepinephrine.

Elavil (amitriptyline) has an established efficacy in the management of chronic pain. For years, Anafranil (clomipramine) was the drug of choice in the treatment of obsessive-compulsive disorder, but it was eventually supplanted by the selective serotonin reuptake inhibitors. Desyrel (trazodone) has proven to be quite effective in the management of depression associated with concomitant anxiety and insomnia.

Make no mistake, the cyclics are indeed effective antidepressants. In fact, they were preferred treatments from the 1950s to the 1990s. Unfortunately, the cyclics are fraught with side effects that render them intolerable for many patients:

- As a class, they tend to be dangerous in overdose and can enhance the sedative effects of alcohol.
- They are sedating, in that they inhibit the effects of histamine, similar to the actions of Benadryl (diphenhydramine).
- They can cause annoying side effects—such as dry mouth, blurred vision, constipation, urinary retention and confusion—because they block the actions of the neurotransmitter acetylcholine.
- They can cause orthostatic hypotension, a drop in standing blood pressure.
- There is a risk of tachycardia, or rapid heart rate.
- Weight gain is associated with a metabolic slowdown in carbohydrate and fat metabolism. In some individuals, weight gain is contributed to by an increased craving for sweets and fats.
- A decrease in libido and an inability to perform sexually is linked to the serotonin effects of these antidepressants.

SELECTIVE SEROTONIN REUPTAKE INHIBITORS (SSRIs)

The SSRIs are indeed popular—one of the most famous ending up on the cover of *Newsweek* magazine, as noted above. Prozac (fluoxetine) was the first of a new class of drugs called selective serotonin reuptake inhibitors (SSRIs) that went on to become the most prescribed class of antidepressants. By today's treatment standards, more than half of all new antidepressant prescriptions are for an SSRI.

These medications work by selectively blocking or inhibiting the reuptake of the neurotransmitter serotonin. In addition to Prozac, other SSRIs include Zoloft (sertraline), Paxil (paroxetine), Celexa (citalopram), Lexapro (escitalopram) and Luvox (fluvoxamine).

As a class, the SSRIs are better tolerated than the cyclics. They have the advantage of once-a-day dosing and are much safer in overdose than the cyclic agents. There is, however, insufficient data to support the efficacy of SSRIs over the cyclic antidepressants.

Side effects of the SSRIs tend to be related to an increase in serotonin activity, and they tend to be fewer than those of the older cyclic antidepressants. SSRI side effects also tend to be transient, with the exception of weight gain and sexual dysfunction, which are associated with long-term use. The main side effects include:

- Increased anxiety
- Sedation
- Significant insomnia (reported in up to 20 percent of cases)
- Sexual dysfunction
- Weight gain, but less than that associated with older antidepressants. One study noted an average weight gain of four pounds over a six-month period.

Discontinuing SSRIs is best done gradually to spare patients unnecessary upset. Abruptly stopping an SSRI is linked to a withdrawal syndrome in which some patients report "electric shock sensations" in the hands and feet accompanied by painful "brain zaps" in the head. Although unpleasant, these effects are not considered dangerous to either the brain or the extremities.

SEROTONIN AND NOREPINEPHRINE REUPTAKE INHIBITORS (SNRIs)

SNRIs are considered dual-action antidepressants. That is, they inhibit or block the reuptake of both serotonin and norepinephrine.

The model drug in this category is Effexor (venlafaxine). In 1994, this was marketed as "Prozac with a punch." The "punch" refers to Effexor's effect on norepinephrine. At doses of less than 150 mg, Effexor (venlafaxine) is essentially no different from a typical SSRI. But at doses of 150 mg or higher, Effexor is said to block the reuptake of serotonin and norepinephrine.

Cymbalta (duloxetine) became available in 2004. Both Cymbalta (duloxetine) and Effexor (venlafaxine) are believed to be more effective than the SSRIs in managing severe depression. But unlike Effexor, Cymbalta is also approved for the treatment of diabetic neuropathic pain. It is also demonstrating promising results in the management of chronic pain and stress urinary incontinence.

Effexor (venlafaxine) may cause high blood pressure, especially at doses of 225 mg per day or higher. Patients taking Effexor at these doses are encouraged to monitor their blood pressure a minimum of once per day. The effects of Cymbalta (duloxetine) on blood pressure are not well established. Otherwise, the side effects of the SNRIs are similar to those of the SSRIs.

The newest entry into the antidepressant market is Pristiq (desvenlafaxine). Pristiq (desvenlafaxine), is in the SNRI category of antidepressants and is manufactured by the Wyeth Corporation. This drug received FDA approval in March, 2008. Faced with the fact that Wyeth is losing patent protection for its top-selling antidepressant Effexor XR (venlafaxine XR), the company needed a brand product that would potentially replace some of the revenue loss when Effexor XR goes generic in 2010. Sales of Effexor XR in 2007 hovered around 3.8 billion dollars (*New York Times*, March, 2008).

Wyeth claims that Pristiq has distinct advantages over Effexor XR. Among them are that patients can begin taking Pristiq at the therapeutic dose of 50 milligrams thereby circumventing the "start low, go slow" gradual increases associated with determining the appropriate dose for an individual. Another advantage of Pristiq, according to Dr. Philip Ninan, a Wyeth vice president for neuroscience, is that Pristiq is unlikely to interact with other medications metabolized by the liver.

But several analysts are skeptical of Pristiq, claiming that it has not set itself apart from other antidepressants on the market, and that its release appeared primarily to have the drug serve as a "patent extender" for Effexor XR. This is because Pristiq is a primary active metabolite of Effexor, meaning Pristiq is the chemical compound that results after Effexor is taken, metabolized and processed by the body. Interestingly, Wyeth is also seeking FDA approval for the use of Pristiq in decreasing menopausal related hot flashes. The most commonly reported side effect of Pristiq is nausea. Also, blood pressure needs to be monitored.

NOREPINEPHRINE REUPTAKE INHIBITORS (NRIs)

The antidepressants Strattera (atomoxetine) and Vestra (reboxetine) selectively block the reuptake of norepinephrine. Strattera (atomoxetine) is FDA-approved for the treatment of ADHD. Although pharmacologically considered an antidepressant, it is not FDA-approved for the treatment of depression. Vestra (reboxetine) remains unavailable for use in the United States, but is available in Europe. NRIs are noted for providing an energy boost, as well as for decreasing distractibility and improving attention span.

Remeron (mirtazapine), works indirectly on norepinephrine and serotonin as did Serzone (nefazodone) before it was removed from the U.S. drug market by its manufacturer Bristol-Meyers Squibb in June, 2004. Serzone (nefazodone) was linked to dozens of liver failures in Europe, Australia, New Zealand and Canada, and was taken off those markets prior to its removal in the United States.

Remeron (mirtazapine) seems to help with the anxiety and sleep problems common to depression. With Remeron, however, weight gain due to an increase in appetite is very common. In rare instances, Remeron (mirtazapine) also decreases white blood-cell count.

MONOAMINE OXIDASE INHIBITORS (MAOIs)

Monoamine oxidase inhibitors (MAOIs) were first developed in the 1950s and today are rarely used, due to their numerous and potentially serious drug-drug interactions and drug-food interactions.

Monoamine oxidase is an enzyme that circulates in the central nervous system to metabolize neurotransmitters at presynaptic nerve endings. The antidepressant properties of the MAOIs are linked to the fact that these agents inhibit the actions of this enzyme. Two common MAOIs are Parnate (tranylcypromine) and Nardil (phenelzine).

A monoamine oxidase inhibitor transdermal delivery system (patch) called Emsam (selegiline) is now available. Pharmacokinetically, the patch delivers its active ingredient by way of absorption through the skin. Purportedly, this delivery system is associated with fewer side effects when compared with the oral administration of the MAOIs.

MAOIs are linked to a host of drug-drug interactions. For example, an extremely dangerous and possibly fatal interaction may occur when Demerol (meperidine) is combined with an MAOI. Patients taking an MAOI also need to be cautioned about the use of over-the-counter drugs, such as the common cough remedy dextromethorpan.

Potentially serious drug-food interactions also make the MAOIs problematic. Tyramine is an amino acid that plays a role in maintaining blood pressure and is metabolized by monoamine oxidase. Foods containing tyramine, if combined with MAOIs, can result in a hypertensive crisis as arterial blood pressure rises, at times suddenly. Patients should be provided with a list of tyramine-containing foods to avoid while taking MAOIs. Also, MAOIs should *never* be combined with SSRIs for fear of the development of "serotonin syndrome." Characterized by fever, profuse sweating, rigidity, twitching, rapid pulse, high blood pressure, confusion and altered consciousness, this syndrome can result in a coma or even death.

Figure 5-1. Food Products that Contain Tyramine

Because of potentially serious drug-food interactions—for example, a sudden, dangerous spike in blood pressure—the following foods should be avoided while taking monoamine oxidase inhibitor drugs (MAOIs). This is not a complete list, and patients should consult their physicians.

- Alcohol: Beer and ale (including non-alcoholic varieties), red wine, port, whiskey, liqueurs, vermouth, sherry, Riesling, sauternes.
- Aged cheeses: American, blue, Boursault, brie, camembert, cheddar, Roquefort, Stilton, Swiss, parmesan, processed, mozzarella, gruyere, Romano
- Fish: Smoked, pickled, dried or fermented. This list includes herring and fish roe, such as caviar.
- Aged or cured meats: Including sausages, bologna, salami, pepperoni, game meats and canned meats
- Meat tenderizer, meat extracts
- Fermented bean curd products: tofu, miso soup
- Fava beans
- Fruits and vegetables: Overripe avocados and figs; raisins, bananas, red plums, tomatoes, spinach and eggplant
- Sour cream, yogurt
- Sauerkraut
- Shrimp paste
- Brewer's yeast or yeast extracts
- Powdered and liquid protein dietary supplements
- Vitamins and supplements containing yeast

ATYPICAL ANTIDEPRESSANTS

Atypicals don't fit specifically into an antidepressant "family" as the others do. In this category, the antidepressant of note is Wellbutrin (bupropion). Since its release in the late 1980s, the mechanism of action has at times been described as sketchy. Wellbutrin (bupropion) exerts no effect on serotonin and has only a modest effect on the norepinephrine system. This medication's considerable effectiveness as an antidepressant is likely linked to its action on dopamine nerve cells. It can be considered a dopamine and norepinephrine reuptake inhibitor (DNRI). Some studies suggest that Wellbutrin (bupropion) does not destabilize the moods of bipolar patients, resulting in fewer of them tipping into mania or rapid cycling.

According to the National Institute of Mental Health, as many as 60 percent of depressed individuals who are unresponsive to other antidepressants improve on Wellbutrin (bupropion). This is why it is commonly used in Treatment Resistant Depression (discussed in Chapter 6).

The primary side effects of Wellbutrin (bupropion) are anxiety and insomnia. The insomnia can be significant to the point of requiring management with a prescription hypnotic (sleep-aid). Wellbutrin (bupropion) is associated with few, if any, sexual side effects. But there is a seizure risk at doses greater than 400 mg a day, which is why for the most part it is contraindicated in seizure disorder. This medication is also contraindicated in alcohol withdrawal, since that condition can lead to seizures, as is also the case in patients with eating disorders.

Zyban (bupropion HCL) is a slow-release form of Wellbutrin that has been approved by the FDA as a treatment for smoking cessation. A dosage of 150 mg twice daily is recommended to help people abstain from smoking and avoid subsequent weight gain.

WHAT YOU AND YOUR CLIENTS NEED TO KNOW

Depression is a real illness, not a character flaw or a weakness. Clinicians should do their best to "destigmatize" depression, emphasizing that it is an illness no different from diabetes or hypertension. Additionally, depression is highly responsive to appropriate treatment.

Clients should be educated about the possible adverse effects of antidepressants, how long it typically takes to see improvement (discussed earlier), and the importance of taking medication properly, including avoiding abrupt discontinuation. They should also be told that if one medication is unsuccessful, others may be tried until an appropriate one is found to produce the desired therapeutic effect.

CASE STUDY: DEPRESSION—"I JUST DON'T HAVE ANY ENERGY LATELY."

Rhetta is a 25-year-old woman who presents to her family practitioner for her annual physical examination and Pap smear. She is a single heterosexual female, a vegetarian who does not drink alcohol or smoke, and tests negative for substance abuse. She is currently taking Lo-Ovral-28, an oral contraceptive, one tablet daily. She relates a 14-pound weight loss in the last two months. She also complains of a lack of energy, but she has trouble falling asleep. She works part-time as a youth director at a local church while pursuing a master's degree in art at a local university. She complains of the stress generated by her demanding job and attending school at the same time. She has had considerable difficulty concentrating over the past four weeks and has not turned in a class project that was due last week. Being a talented artist, some of her work has been on display at statewide festivals and exhibits. Presently, however, she expresses little interest in painting and is thinking about leaving graduate school. Rhetta is the youngest of four siblings, with alcoholic parents. When she was eight years old, her mother died of liver cirrhosis. She was placed in foster care in the fourth grade. An older sister is taking Zoloft for depression.

Rhetta is appropriately dressed with clean clothes. She sobs at times during the interview. Her affect is sad, her mood is depressed, and she admits to having suicidal ideation but no specific plan. She is oriented to person, place, and time, but she displays some recent memory deficits accompanied by poor concentration. She is of above average intelligence with satisfactory insight and judgment, and she denies hearing voices or having other hallucinations.

Diagnostic Considerations

Rhetta's treating physician concludes that she is experiencing a major depressive episode. Though this depression seems to have developed due to her difficulty in adjusting to work and school demands, symptomatically she is experiencing physiological symptoms as well. As a result, her doctor recommends she try an antidepressant. She agrees to do so and is started on Zoloft (sertraline), 25 mg daily for one week, then increasing to 50 mg daily for one week, and then 100 mg daily thereafter. The physician explains the common side effects associated with Zoloft (sertraline), that it may take three to four weeks for symptoms to improve, and that she should do her best to not miss any doses. He also mentions that since she has a sister taking Zoloft (sertraline), it may prove to be a good choice for her also.

Treatment Course

Rhetta responds quite favorably to this Zoloft regimen. Although she does experience some of the side effects her doctor mentioned, they are manageable. After six weeks, practically all of the clinical depression symptoms have abated. She is instructed to remain on the Zoloft (sertraline) for another six months and to then schedule a follow-up appointment for re-evaluation.

DOSAGE RANGE CHART — ANTIDEPRESSANTS

BRAND NAME	GENERIC NAME	CLASS	DAILY DOSAGE RANGE *
Anafranil	clomipramine	cyclic	150 mg - 250mg
Celexa	citalopram	SSRI	20 mg - 80 mg
Cymbalta	duloxetine	SNRI	20 mg - 80 mg
Desyrel	trazodone	cyclic	150 mg - 400 mg
Effexor	venlafaxine	SNRI	75 mg - 350 mg
Effexor XR	venlafaxine XR	SNRI	75 mg - 350 mg
Elavil	amitriptyline	cyclic	100 mg - 300 mg
Emsam (patch)	selegiline	MAOI	6 mg - 12 mg
Lexapro	escitalopram	SSRI	10 mg - 40 mg
Luvox	fluvoxamine	SSRI	100 mg - 400 mg
Nardil	phenelzine	MAOI	45 mg - 60 mg
Norpramin	desipramine	cyclic	150 mg - 300 mg
Pamelor	nortriptyline	cyclic	75 mg - 150 mg
Parnate	tranylcypromine	MAOI	20 mg - 60 mg
Paxil	paroxetine	SSRI	20 mg - 50 mg
Prozac	fluoxetine	SSRI	20 mg - 80 mg
Remeron	mirtazapine	atypical	15 mg - 45 mg
Sarafem	fluoxetine	SSRI	20 mg - 80 mg
Sinequan	doxepin	cyclic	150 mg - 300 mg
Strattera	atomoxetine	NRI	60 mg – 120 mg
Tofranil	imipramine	cyclic	150 mg - 300 mg
Wellbutrin SR	bupropion SR	atypical	150 mg – 300 mg
Wellbutrin LA	bupropion LA	atypical	150 mg – 300 mg
Zoloft	sertraline	SSRI	50 mg - 200 mg

* Suggested adult dose

Note: Dosage ranges may vary depending on source, and may also vary according to age.

6

IF THE DEPRESSION CONTINUES, THEN WHAT?

Treatment-resistant depression (TRD) is exactly what it sounds like—a depression that is mostly or partially resistant to treatment. One definition of TRD is a depression that has failed to respond to a course of treatment over a minimum of four to six weeks of two or more antidepressants. Some estimates place this at 10 percent to 20 percent of all cases of depression. For patients receiving only one antidepressant over an adequate trial period, the rate of failure to respond to treatment can be as high as 30 percent.

What contributes to treatment resistance when attempting to manage depression pharmacologically? There may be an undiagnosed or misdiagnosed medical disorder. Also, there may be a co-occurring psychiatric disorder that either complicates or exacerbates the depression. In these instances, a re-evaluation of a patient's physical and mental condition may be warranted. There may be other prescription drugs prescribed that are known to cause or potentially worsen depression. Other factors affecting treatment response are substance abuse and eating disorders. Always screen for alcohol use in cases of TRD.

Research into the efficacy of treating depression through the use of one antidepressant alone—known as monotherapy—continues to raise a specter of doubt. The most sobering statistics regarding TRD come from the National Institute of Mental Health:

- 55 percent to 65 percent of depressed subjects utilizing one antidepressant alone demonstrate a partial or even no response.

- 35 percent to 45 percent do enter into active remission, but of these, a full one third continue to display residual symptoms of depression.

Conclusion: Monotherapy is not adequate for most depressed subjects, particularly long term.

Examined more simply, of those who utilize antidepressant monotherapy, one third shows improvement, one third demonstrates a partial response, and one third shows no improvement at all. This indicates that as many as two thirds of all depressed patients using monotherapy demonstrate only a partial response or no response.

PHARMACOLOGICAL AUGMENTATION STRATEGIES FOR TREATING TRD

Augmentation refers to the addition of medication from different chemical classes or to the combination of antidepressants. The goal of any augmentation treatment strategy is to enhance the actions of norepinephrine, serotonin, dopamine and even GABA enough to facilitate mood improvement.

Drugs that can be added to antidepressants include:

- Lithium: The addition of lithium to the treatment regimens of nonresponsive patients has been investigated in repeated controlled studies. It is frequently the first-choice treatment for patients who have failed to respond to antidepressant monotherapy.
- Thyroid supplements: Because adequate thyroid function is so important to metabolism and mood, adding thyroid supplements, such as Synthroid and Levothroid (both levothyroxine), may prove beneficial, particularly in menopausal or perimenopausal women.
- Stimulants: Adding stimulants typically employed in the management of attention deficit disorder, such as Adderall (dextroamphetamine/amphetamine) or Ritalin (methylphenidate), can be effective in treating TRD.
- Atypical antipsychotics: Some of these antipsychotic medications—including Zyprexa (olanzapine), Seroquel (quetiapine), Geodon (ziprasidone) and Abilify (aripiprazole)—also possess antidepressant properties.

- L-methylfolate. Deplin (l-methylfolate): This is a folic acid type of derivative that became available to the U.S. market in 2007. Deplin (l-methylfolate) helps normalize amounts of the neurotransmitters norepinephrine, serotonin and dopamine when used in conjunction with antidepressants. Depressed patients consistently have lower serum folate concentrations.

Antidepressants that can be used in combination with each other include: SSRIs + Wellbutrin; Remeron + Effexor; Remeron + SSRIs; Effexor + Wellbutrin; and Effexor + SSRIs.

An increasingly common antidepressant combination is Cymbalta + Wellbutrin (duloxetine and bupropion). This combination can stimulate neurotransmission in all three nerve chemical systems, increasing the availability of norepinephrine, serotonin and dopamine. It is considered by some to be the most effective antidepressant combination for TRD.

WHAT ELSE CAN YOU DO?

- Monitor dosage: It is no secret that many depressed individuals are under-medicated. Sometimes a prescriber will need to adjust the dose to the FDA-approved maximum before results will be seen.
- Monitor compliance: Patients skip doses of their medications, particularly antidepressants, for a number of reasons, including the "stigma" associated with a diagnosis of depression. Others are side effects and the cost of prescriptions. (See Appendix III. Medication Noncompliance.)

When pharmacological augmentation strategies don't work—either by adding drugs from a different class or combining them in typically effective pairs—other strategies need to be considered. These include "mechanical" strategies that warrant referrals to physicians or other skilled professionals knowledgeable in administering or performing these procedures. These strategies include:

- Electroconvulsive Treatment (ECT): ECT came to pass as a procedure for treating depression when it was discovered that after a seizure, patients often reported an improvement in mood and affect. In seizure disorder, neurotransmission is enhanced as a result of the repeated firing of neurons. ECT mimics a seizure, in this case an electrical therapeutic seizure lasting about 15 seconds.

ECT was in widespread use in the United States and England in the 1940s and 1950s, but experienced a decline from the 1950s to the 1970s with the advent of antidepressant medications. The procedure has been refined over the years and is now performed under general anesthesia. It appears to carry no more risks than those of general anesthesia, and numerous reports confirm that ECT does not cause structural brain damage. The biggest single drawback to multiple treatments of ECT is memory loss, which can be either short-term or long- term. Still, ECT remains a somewhat controversial procedure due to sensationalism in movies and literature, and it is generally used only in those patients with severe depression who have not responded to antidepressants. ECT is an FDA-approved procedure.

- <u>Repetitive Transcranial Magnetic Stimulation (rTMS):</u> This is an exciting new tool in the research on brain function, but at this point it is under review by the FDA with regard to treatment for depression in the United States. (It was approved for use in Canada in 2002.) Electrical activity in the brain is influenced by a pulsed magnetic field that is passed through a coil of wire encased in plastic and held close to the head. This magnetic field painlessly penetrates the scalp and skull, focusing on specific areas of the brain associated with mood disorders. The stimulation is made at regular intervals, thus the term "repetitive" TMS.

In studies, rTMS appears to change brain activity beyond the duration of the actual procedure. Also, the procedure differs from ECT in that it stimulates the brain in a focal manner, thereby preventing the grand mal seizure and transitory memory loss associated with ECT. In October, 2008 the FDA cleared the NeuroStar TMS Therapy system by Neuronetics, Inc. for the treatment of depression.

- Vagal Nerve Stimulation (VNS): This mechanical strategy is an invasive procedure, initially used in epileptic patients and recently FDA-approved for TRD. VNS involves the implantation of a device called an NCP System in the upper chest. Then, electrodes are connected to the left cervical vagus nerve, through which electrical signals are delivered. This can facilitate neurotransmission, thus making this procedure potentially effective for the management of TRD.

7

RUNAWAY NOREPINEPHRINE AND NEURONS GONE WILD

Once devastating and strangely alluring to its sufferers, bipolar disorder was first dubbed "manic-depressive insanity" by 19th-century psychiatrist Emil Kraepelin. Today bipolar disorder is characterized mainly by its unpredictable cycle of intense mood swings, typically fluctuating between the two poles of mania and depression.

Some 5.7 million American adults, or 2.6 percent of all, have bipolar disorder in any given year, according to the National Institute of Mental Health. Although bipolar disorder affects fewer people than unipolar depression, it can be more destructive to relationships, health, finances and careers. This is due to its related disruptive behaviors, which include delusional thinking, binges and engaging in reckless activities.

More recently referred to as manic-depressive illness, the bipolar spectrum disorders are classified as mood disorders like major depressive illness and dysthymia. All are characterized by a cycling pattern of mood, behavior and thought processes that fluctuate between mania (or hypomania) and depression.

Mania, according to the current DSM-IV TR, is defined as a "distinct period of abnormally and persistently elevated, expansive, or irritable mood lasting at least seven days (or any duration if hospitalization is necessary)." Since mania rarely occurs as a stand-alone clinical condition, its presence usually leads to a bipolar diagnosis. Characteristic symptoms of mania include racing thoughts, pressured speech, grandiosity, distractibility, insomnia, flight of ideas and an increase in risk-taking behavior.

Table 7-1. Signs and Symptoms of Manic and Depressive Episodes

Manic Episode Symptoms:	**Depressive Episode Symptoms:**
• Increased energy, activity, restlessness	• Lasting sad, anxious or empty mood
• Excessively "high," overly good, euphoric mood	• Feelings of hopelessness or pessimism
• Extreme irritability	• Restlessness or irritability
• Racing thoughts, talking very fast, jumping from one idea to another	• Decreased energy, a feeling of fatigue or being "slowed down"
• Distractibility; inability to concentrate; poor judgment; spending sprees	• Difficulty concentrating, remembering and making decisions
• Unrealistic beliefs in one's abilities and powers	• Thoughts of death or suicide, or suicide attempts
• Little sleep needed	• Sleeping too much, or can't sleep
• A lasting period of behavior that is different from usual	• Change in appetite and/or unintended weight loss or gain
• Increased sexual drive ties	• Loss of interest or pleasure in activi- once enjoyed, including sex
• Abuse of drugs, particularly cocaine, alcohol and sleeping medications	• Chronic pain or other persistent bodily symptoms not caused by physical illness or injury
• Provocative, intrusive or aggressive behavior	• Feelings of guilt, worthlessness, or helplessness
• Denial that anything is wrong	

DATA: *"Signs and Symptoms of Mania and Depression," National Institute of Mental Health*

Hypomania is a mild to moderate level of mania, a period of elevated mood and uncommon energy that lasts at least four days. It differs from full-blown mania in that symptoms do not cause significant functional impairment in personal, social or occupational interactions; nor is hospitalization likely to be an issue. Often described by patients as pleasurable and exciting, hypomania brings an attendant feeling of enthusiasm and charisma with an apparent free flow of ideas and creativity. Although hypomania may feel satisfying to the person experiencing it, without proper treatment it can escalate into full mania or switch to depression.

The pattern of the mood swings determines which of the three types of bipolar disorder is occurring:

Bipolar I: This disorder is characterized by one or more manic or hypomanic episodes with one or more episodes of major depression. In bipolar I, moods can swing dramatically in both directions. The depressions are severe, and the manias may be out of control. Episodes of depression in bipolar I must meet the criteria for major depression as outlined in the current edition of the DSM-IV TR.

Bipolar II: Here, mood swings involve a severe, full-blown depression as in bipolar I, but the "high" episodes do not reach true mania. This disorder is characterized by the presence of one or more major depressive episodes in combination with at least one episode of hypomania. Bipolar II disorder can be difficult to distinguish from major depression, and at one time the two used to be thought of as variants of the same condition. In fact, the predominant symptomatic presentation is depressive in nature, and an exact definition of what constitutes hypomania can be open to interpretation. Clinicians differ in their capacity and ability to accurately assess for it. DSM-IV TR criteria require that symptoms of hypomania be present for at least four days.

Cyclothymia: This disorder is characterized by mood swings that last for at least two years, with less intense highs and lows than those that occur in bipolar I and II. That is, the episodes do not reach true mania or major depression. However, this can make cyclothymia difficult to diagnose.

Cyclothymia is a chronic disorder, and patients typically have a history of numerous hypomanic and depressive episodes. Although characterized by "mild" mood swings, cyclothymia can cause significant distress in daily living, due to the abrupt changes from joy to sadness, difficulty sleeping, and problems maintaining the enthusiasm needed to complete projects. Arguably, a diagnosis of cyclothymia may serve as a warning sign of the possible future emergence of a bipolar disorder.

Rapid cycling is defined as a type of bipolar illness in which an individual experiences four or more episodes of mania and/or major depression within a 12-month period. Some individuals cycle from manic episode to manic episode, while others cycle from depressive episode to depressive episode. Still others have mixed episodes that include symptoms of both mania and depression. Episodes can occur over a month, week, or day. Approximately 20 percent of bipolar patients are rapid cyclers; of these, 80 percent are women.

ETIOLOGY

Bipolar disorder is a biologically based illness. Since its first description in 1898, numerous theories have been suggested to explain the disorder's origins. Today, two main approaches are the Kindling Theory and the Catecholamine Theory.

The Kindling Theory hypothesizes that some psychiatric symptoms are a result of biochemical changes in the "emotional brain" that cause nerve cells to become excited. This process causes more neurons to "fire," and the more they fire, the greater the possibility that neurotransmission is going to increase, setting off a constellation of observable and diagnosable symptoms. Left unchecked and untreated, mood fluctuations are likely to occur more often, resulting in the brain becoming increasingly sensitized and the destructive pathways inside the central nervous system being strengthened. According to this theory, a mood disorder is like a fire: Just as a large log burns only with enough time and kindling, so does one unstable mood episode leads to more frequent and more severe episodes in the future.

The Catecholamine Theory suggests that bipolar illness is linked to an increase in cerebrospinal fluid levels of norepinephrine. Catecholamines, such as the naturally occurring chemical compounds norepinephrine and epinephrine (adrenalin), prepare the body for "fight or flight." This theory, proposed by U.S. psychiatrist Joseph Schildkraut, emerged in the 1960s. Schildkraut was particularly interested in norepinephrine. He suggested that a deficiency of this neurotransmitter at receptor sites caused depression, while increased levels caused mania. The catecholamine theory demonstrated how pharmacology offered a rational approach to the biology of the brain, and Schildkraut's work is credited with increasing the understanding of the role that biology plays in diagnosing and treating psychiatric illnesses.

OTHER CAUSES

Medical conditions that are linked to increased excitability of neurons can also be associated with mania. These include:

- Central nervous system trauma
- Hyperthyroidism, an endocrine system disorder
- Infectious diseases
- Central nervous system tumors
- Seizure disorders

In addition, some medications themselves can potentially stimulate neurotransmission of the "emotional chemicals," particularly norepinephrine and dopamine. These medications include:

- Psychostimulants, especially amphetamines
- Antidepressants, especially the cyclics
- The corticosteroid prednisone, in high doses
- Thyroid hormones

SUICIDE

Bipolar patients can be at increased risk for suicide, especially in the earlier stages of the illness. Signs and symptoms to watch for, according to the National Institute of Mental Health, include:

- Talking about feeling suicidal or wanting to die
- Feeling hopeless, believing that nothing will ever change or improve
- Feeling helpless, believing that nothing one does can make a difference
- Feeling like a burden to family and friends

- Abusing alcohol or drugs
- Suddenly putting affairs in order. For example, organizing finances, giving away possessions, etc.
- Writing a suicide note
- Putting oneself in a dangerous situation

Table 7-2. Famous People with Bipolar Disorder
Ludwig von Beethoven: composer
Art Buchwald: writer, humorist
Winston Churchill: British prime minister
Vincent van Gogh: artist
Graham Greene: author
George Fredrick Handel: composer
Jimi Hendrix: rock musician
Moss Hart: actor, director, playwright
Vivien Leigh: actress
Gustav Mahler: composer
Sylvia Plath: poet
Edgar Allen Poe: author
Robert Schumann: composer
Robert Louis Stevenson: author
August Strindberg: playwright, novelist
Mark Twain: humorist, author
Virginia Woolf: author

8

MOOD-STABILIZING AGENTS

Lithium was the first mood-stabilizing medication approved by the FDA for the treatment of acute mania and hypomania. It might well be the "gold standard" in the treatment of mania, as well as for the maintenance treatment of bipolar I and II. Although lithium has drawbacks, it is considered a first-line agent. It is generally safe and effective when carefully monitored and its side effects appropriately managed.

Two other medication classes with mood-stabilizing properties used to treat bipolar disorders are the anticonvulsants and the atypical antipsychotics. These medications are often used in combination with psychotherapy for a significant and positive impact on this biologically based illness.

LITHIUM

The mood-stabilizing properties of lithium were first noted in the 1800s, when physicians used it for not only treating anxiety, but also gout and seizures. In 1949, an Australian psychiatrist, John Cade, published the first paper on lithium's usefulness for treating acute mania. In his experiments, Cade had earlier observed that lithium had a calming effect on guinea pigs. He then tried it on human subjects and found their mania subsided within a week. It took a while, however, for lithium to gain acceptance in American medicine; government approval did not come until 1970. Then increased marketing of the drug quickly followed under the brand names Eskalith and Lithobid.

Today, more than 50 years later, lithium's workings are still unclear. One theory is that lithium normalizes mania initially through its effects on norepinephrine. When fight or flight is activated, synaptic levels of norepinephrine tend to increase. According to this theory, lithium acts as a fight-or-flight deactivator by increasing norepinephrine reuptake. Lithium's effect on serotonin is theorized to be responsible for its role in managing depressive episodes of bipolar disorder. Because some bipolar patients demonstrate low concentrations of serotonin, lithium may contribute to enhancing the actions of serotonin by increasing levels of tryptophan, a building block of serotonin. Lithium has well documented efficacy in preventing relapse in bipolar disorder.

Lithium reduces the risk of suicide and suicide attempts associated with bipolar disorder, though it does not reduce the risk to levels in the general population. This is important, because about 1 percent of those with bipolar disorder attempt suicide each year.

One drawback to lithium is its slow onset of action: It typically requires five to 14 days, with full stabilization taking up to several months.

Another drawback is lithium's narrow therapeutic index, meaning the therapeutic dose is close to toxic. Most patients must reach a level between 1.0 and 1.2 milliequivalents per liter (mEq/L) to see results. However, the toxic level can begin around 1.5 mEq, even lower. For this reason, lithium requires careful blood-level monitoring.

Generally speaking, the starting dose of lithium is 600 mg to 900 mg daily, administered in divided doses. During acute manic states, daily doses can range from 1200 mg to 2400 mg, with most patients requiring 600 mg to 1800 mg daily after stabilization.

It is recommended that blood-level monitoring be done once every seven days for the first few weeks, then once ever three months after stabilization.

Laboratory tests to check thyroid and kidney function are warranted before lithium treatment begins. Lithium use can lead to a decrease in thyroid production, so it may be useful to obtain a yearly thyroid stimulating hormone (TSH) level to check for this. Symptoms of hypothyroidism include weight gain, fatigue, dry skin and intolerance to cold. It is generally not necessary to stop the lithium, since providing additional thyroid hormone in a daily oral preparation can easily manage decreased thyroid function.

Baseline kidney-function testing is also recommended prior to the initiation of lithium use. Lithium bypasses liver metabolism and depends solely on the kidney for excretion from the body. In the absence of healthy kidney functioning, lithium levels can rise rapidly, and toxicity then becomes a major issue. Though there is concern regarding lithium use and kidney damage, such damage is for the most part rare.

Recommended laboratory tests include:

- Na (Sodium)
- Ca (Calcium)
- P (Phosphorous)
- EKG
- Creatinine
- Urinalysis
- Complete Blood Count
- Thyroid Function

POSSIBLE SIDE EFFECTS

Lithium's side effects range from those that are relatively benign and temporary to more serious ones that can lead to toxicity, coma, even death.

Table 8-1. Side Effects of Lithium

Most Common:	Most Severe:
Thirst	Hypothyroidism
Excessive urination	Kidney dysfunction
Weight gain	Confusion
Nausea, vomiting, diarrhea	Coma
Aggravation of acne	

Common side effects include nausea, diarrhea, vomiting, thirst, excessive urination, weight gain and fine-hand tremor. A benign, reversible increase in white blood cell count frequently occurs with lithium use. This ordinarily does not rise to clinical significance; nor does it require lithium discontinuation. Chronic use side effects include hypothyroidism, goiter, and rarely, kidney damage. And signs of toxicity include lethargy, ataxia, slurred speech, shock, delirium, coma and death.

Lithium elimination from the body is affected by excessive sodium loss. Sodium loss through dehydration, diarrhea, increased perspiration or diuretic medication use can trigger lithium retention in the body that could reach toxic levels. As such, baseline kidney function tests are warranted, and regular monitoring is imperative.

ANTICONVULSANTS

Another class of mood stabilizers used to manage bipolar disorder is the anticonvulsants, utilized for more 35 years in the management of seizure disorder. Similar to lithium, the exact functioning of how anticonvulsants treat bipolar disorder remains unclear. The chief suspect, however, is the anticonvulsants' ability to enhance the actions of GABA, the primary inhibitory neurotransmitter in the central nervous system.

Several anticonvulsants have demonstrated efficacy and are the most widely prescribed. These include Depakote (divalproex), Lamictal (lamotrigine), Tegretol (carbamazepine) and Topamax (topiramate).

Depakote (divalproex) is considered—like lithium—a first-line agent for mania and is the likely agent of choice for rapid cycling. Several studies have indicated that it works more quickly than lithium and may be better tolerated. Depakote (divalproex) is also excellent for treating rage reactions and extreme mood instability in bipolar disorder, and disruptive behaviors associated with conduct disorder, borderline personality disorder, autism and attention deficit hyperactivity disorder. The drug is typically ineffective in the treatment of bipolar depression.

The main side effects of Depakote (divalproex) include sedation, dizziness, drowsiness, blurred vision and coordination problems. Gastrointestinal side effects include nausea, vomiting, diarrhea, and abdominal pain. Taking the medication with food or milk may lessen these. Depakote (divalproex) can also cause interference with blood clotting; liver toxicity in children (although this is primarily associated with those taking multiple psychiatric medications); weight gain in approximately 50 percent of patients seems to be dose-related; and pancreatitis, with its primary symptom of abdominal pain. Any reports of abdominal pain should be immediately referred to a physician. Another possible side effect of Depakote (divalproex) is polycystic ovarian syndrome (PCOS) in women of childbearing age, which can lead to decreased fertility, weight gain, menstrual irregularities and endocrine problems such as excessive hair growth.

Lamictal (lamotrigine) is approved for acute and maintenance treatment of bipolar illness. Because of its serotonin effects, it is considered first-line for the treatment of the depressive end of a mood swing as opposed to the manic phase. This renders it a suitable augmentation agent with lithium or Depakote, which treat the manic phase more effectively.

Central nervous system side effects of Lamictal (lamotrigine) include sedation, dizziness, drowsiness, blurred vision and coordination problems. Gastrointestinal side effects include nausea, vomiting, diarrhea and abdominal pain. Taking the medication with food or milk may lessen these.

A potentially serious side effect of Lamictal (lamotrigine) is rash development, including Stevens-Johnson syndrome. This does not necessarily mean that all rashes associated with Lamictal (lamotrigine) use are linked to Stevens-Johnson, but it is something that should be monitored. With Stevens-Johnson, tissue undergoes necrolysis and takes on the appearance of a Stage Three or Stage Four burn. Rash development, which occurs in about 10 percent of patients, seems to be related to how fast this medication is started and subsequently titrated upward. Current clinical guidelines recommend that lamotrigine doses be gradually increased to typical daily maximums of 100 mg to 200 mg over a six-week period. If any manifestation of a rash appears, this drug should be discontinued immediately and a physician consulted.

Tegretol (carbamazepine) is effective for mania but is generally considered a second-line agent to Depakote (divalproex). Like Depakote (divalproex), Tegretol (carbamazepine) is not effective and unproven in the treatment of bipolar depression. For years it has been a very effective anticonvulsant for use in the management of grand mal seizures. It is still used nowadays to manage aggressive outbursts in children. Central nervous system side effects include sedation, dizziness, drowsiness, blurred vision and coordination problems. Gastrointestinal side effects include nausea, vomiting, diarrhea and abdominal pain. Taking the medication with food or milk may lessen these.

Tegretol (carbamazepine) is also linked to the potentially serious side effect of agranulocytosis, causing a decrease in white blood cell count that can lead to the development of opportunistic infection.

Topamax (topiramate) lacks efficacy in well-controlled studies in the management of bipolar disorder; in effect it has basically failed as a mood stabilizer, unlike the other drugs mentioned here. But it is one of the very few psychotropic medications linked to reversing weight loss caused by other psychotropics. Also, because of its effects on calcium channel signaling and GABA, it is becoming well established in the successful treatment of migraine headaches and has received FDA approval for this. Topamax (topiramate) has also demonstrated some short-term efficacy in alcohol dependence by reducing alcohol cravings after the withdrawal phase.

A potentially significant side effect of Topamax (topiramate) involves cognitive difficulties—cognitive "fog"—as well as memory disturbance and word-finding difficulties. Rare cases of glaucoma and kidney stones have also surfaced.

Table 8-2. Side Effects of Anticonvulsants

Drug	Side Effects
Tegretol (carbamazepine)	• Sedation, dizziness, drowsiness, blurred vision and coordination problems. • Nausea, vomiting, diarrhea and abdominal pain. • Linked to potentially serious side effect of

	agranulocytosis, causing significant decrease in white blood cell count, which can lead to opportunistic infections.
Depakote (divalproex)	• Sedation, dizziness, drowsiness, blurred vision and coordination problems. • Nausea, vomiting, diarrhea and abdominal pain. • Interference with blood clotting; weight gain in approximately 50 percent of patients; pancreatitis; possible liver toxicity in children; polycystic ovarian syndrome (PCOS) in women of childbearing age.
Lamictal (lamotrigine)	• Sedation, dizziness, drowsiness, blurred vision and coordination problems. • Nausea, vomiting, diarrhea, and abdominal pain. • Rash development, including Stevens-Johnson syndrome (potentially serious).
Topamax (topiramate)	• Cognitive difficulties—mental "fog"—as well as memory disturbance and word-finding difficulties. • Rare cases of glaucoma and kidney stones have also surfaced.

OTHER ANTICONVULSANTS

Currently, other anticonvulsants are considered alternative or augmenting agents for bipolar disorder. On the whole, these anticonvulsants lack well-controlled clinical studies supporting their first0line or, in some cases, second-line use in bipolar disorder. These include Neurontin (gabapentin), Gabitril (tiagabine), Trileptal (oxcarbazepine), Felbatol (felbamate), Keppra (levetiracetam) and Lyrica (pregabalin).

ATYPICAL ANTIPSYCHOTICS

Newer, atypical antipsychotics are gaining increasingly widespread acceptance in the management of bipolar disorder. For example, Zyprexa (olanzapine) and Abilify (aripiprazole) are both FDA-approved for acute and maintenance treatment of bipolar mania. Another atypical antipsychotic, Symbyax (olanzapine and fluoxetine), is FDA-approved for the treatment of depressive episodes associated with bipolar disorder. All of the atypical antipsychotics currently available in the United States—with the notable exception of Clozaril (clozapine)—are FDA-approved for acute bipolar mania. (A detailed description of these drugs and their side effects are outlined in Chapter 3.)

WHAT YOU AND YOUR CLIENTS NEED TO KNOW

The pharmacological treatment of bipolar disorder is, to say the least, all over the place, and clinician disagreement as to which medication should be utilized in what particular instance is vast.

The manic phase of bipolar disorder carries a peculiar treatment challenge that most other mental disorders do not: Because mania is a desirable and enjoyable state for many, if not most patients, medication noncompliance is a particular hazard during these episodes. Repeatedly starting and discontinuing mood stabilizers results in erratic blood levels of these medications and a subsequent decrease in their effectiveness. This, in turn, can lead to an increased susceptibility for the occurrence of future episodes, a progressive worsening of symptoms, and a heightened mortality risk. Practitioners should educate their patients on the serious implications of noncompliance with an emphasis on taking these medications as prescribed. (See Appendix III. Medication Noncompliance.)

CASE STUDY: "A VERY IMPORTANT MAN"

Steven is a 25-year-old flooring and carpet sales representative referred to you by his primary care physician. He called your office a day earlier seeking an immediate appointment to discuss his recent bouts of stress, anxiety and sleeplessness. When Steven arrives at your office, he is abrupt, abrasive, and demanding. He tells the administrative assistant that he is a "very important man" who expects to be seen by you "right now." The assistant notifies you of his arrival, but not before he attempts to pass around carpet samples to other clients in the waiting room.

Steven is unshaven, possesses a detectable body odor, and his clothing is wrinkled. He reports that his father has been "in and out of the nut house" as long as he can remember and that one of his older brothers is alcoholic. Steven reveals no other psychiatric history. He is, by self-report, single, never married and without children. He has recently been promoted to senior sales representative at the flooring company owned by his oldest brother.

During the interview, Steven rises from his chair on several occasions and paces incessantly in front of your office window. He states that his recent anxiety and insomnia is entirely his brother's fault. Steven desires to take the family carpet company "global," he continues, but his brother has rejected this plan because "he thinks too small." Steven's speech is pressured, and his thought processes are disorganized and accompanied by a flight of ideas. Considering that Steven's symptoms may be indicative of a manic episode, you refer him to one of the psychiatrists in your agency for additional evaluation.

Diagnostic Considerations

The psychiatrist conducts his own independent assessment and concludes that the inappropriate behavior Steven displayed in the patient waiting area, as well as the overall symptom intensity, warrants medication management. The physician explains to Steven that he has a condition that is well known for the symptoms and behavior he has been experiencing. The psychiatrist suggests a trial of lithium beginning with 300 mg twice daily to be taken at mealtimes. The psychiatrist stressed the importance of monitoring Steven's lithium levels every three to seven days for the first several weeks of treatment, and that the maintenance level to be achieved is 1.0 to 1.2meq/L.

Treatment Course

Over the next six weeks, Steven's lithium dose is increased to 1800 mg daily. Steven responds favorably to lithium treatment, and the doctor suggest he should remain on long-term maintenance management, possibly indefinitely. Throughout the treatment process, Steven's psychiatrist secures all of the appropriate informed consents and engages Steven in a detailed discussion of the possible side effects of lithium use. The physician also emphasizes that for as long as Steven remains in treatment, he will need occasional lithium blood-level monitoring, thyroid function tests and kidney-function tests, probably about once every three months.

DOSAGE RANGE CHART — MOOD STABILIZERS, ANTICONVULSANTS

BRAND NAME	GENERIC NAME	CLASS	DAILY DOSAGE RANGE *
Depakote	divalproex	anticonvulsant	750 mg – 3000 mg
Eskalith	lithium carbonate	mood stabilizer	600 mg – 2400 mg
Gabitril	tiagabine	anticonvulsant	32 mg – 56 mg
Lamictal	lamotrigine	anticonvulsant	100 mg – 200 mg
Neurontin	gabapentin	anticonvulsant	900 mg – 1800 mg
Symbyax	olanzapine/fluoxetine	**	6/25 mg – 12/50 mg
Tegretol	carbamazepine	anticonvulsant	600 mg – 1200 mg
Topamax	topiramate	anticonvulsant	200 mg – 400 mg
Trileptal	oxcarbazepine	anticonvulsant	600 mg – 1200 mg

* Suggested adult dose

** Atypical antipsychotic/antidepressant

Note: Dosage ranges may vary depending on source, and may also vary according to age.

9

THE MANY MANIFESTATIONS OF ANXIETY

More than 40 million Americans suffer from anxiety disorders, making it the most common mental health complaint in the country. Twice as many women as men experience anxiety disorders. It is unknown, however, whether twice as many women actually suffer from anxiety, or whether they simply are more likely to seek treatment and, therefore, be diagnosed.

Anxiety manifestations share four common threads: anxiety as a symptom, avoidance as a behavior, fear and threat (whether real or perceived).

Any thorough differential diagnosis of a patient presenting with anxiety symptoms should account for certain general medical conditions, prescription medications and over-the-counter products that may cause, influence or even exacerbate these symptoms. For this reason, a clinician should *never* conclude that an Axis I clinical anxiety disorder is the case until all possible medical causes have been sufficiently ruled out.

Figure 9-1. Other Factors Influencing Anxiety

These medical conditions, prescription and over-the-counter products are potentially responsible for the emergence of anxiety symptoms.

Medical Conditions

- Angina pectoris: chest pain or discomfort due to coronary heart disease
- Cardiac arrhythmia
- Hypoglycemia: low blood sugar

- Hyperthyroidism
- Premenstrual syndrome

Prescription and Over-the-Counter Products

- Amphetamines, such as Dexedrine or Ritalin
- Appetite suppressants
- Asthma medications, such as Proventil (albuterol), Serevent (salmeterol xinafoate) and Theo-Dur (theophylline)
- Hormone medications, such as oral contraceptives
- Steroids, including prednisone and cortisone
- Nasal decongestants, such as Sudafed (pseudoephedrine)
- Caffeine, found in numerous OTC drugs such as Excedrin, Anacin, No-Doz, Midol and cough remedies; as well as in coffee, tea, caffeinated soft drinks and energy drinks

---

ETIOLOGY

Fight-or-flight is a survival mechanism that has kept the species around for millennia. It is triggered by two closely related chemicals that we have discussed before, norepinephrine and epinephrine. One common depiction of fight-or-flight refers to early man facing a saber-tooth tiger, woolly mammoth or other very real danger of his primitive world. Early man had two choices: He could either confront them (fight) or run from them (flight). Either way, early man's autonomic nervous system prepared physically by dumping noradrenaline, epinephrine and other chemicals into his system. Today, with a dearth of tigers and wooly mammoths in our everyday lives, those stressors have been replaced by events that range from minor aggravations to truly harrowing experiences. Yet the body still reacts the same way it did thousands of years ago.

It is normal to have a fearful reaction when in the presence of actual danger. But an anxiety disorder creates anxiety and panic in the absence of actual danger, when the mind is occupied with a possible future danger, or when the reactions are in excess of what most people would experience in similar circumstances. Physical manifestations of anxiety can number in the dozens, and they run the gamut from annoying to frightening. Sweaty palms are one thing; repeated trips to the emergency room, convinced you are having a heart attack, is another, and one that is likely to interfere with everyday life.

Figure 9-2. Symptoms of Anxiety

- Rapid heart rate (tachycardia) or heart pounding
- Palpitations, or feeling of missed heartbeats
- Shallow breathing
- Hand tremors
- Nervousness, muscle tension
- Fingernail biting, picking at skin
- Shortness of breath
- Difficulty concentrating
- Poor attention, "unfocused"
- Easily startled
- Hypervigilance, constantly "on guard"
- Dizziness
- Nausea
- Insomnia
- Diarrhea, frequent urination, or both
- Sweating
- Visual or aural distortions, feelings of unreality

TYPES OF ANXIETY DISORDERS

Although the DSM-IV TR lists 12 types of anxiety disorders, those discussed here tend to present most often in clinical settings. These disorders are also routinely treated with either nonpharmacological, cognitive-behavioral therapies, medication, or both.

Generalized anxiety disorder (GAD): Defined as "chronic low-level anxiety without panic," this is akin to the low-level depression in dysthymia covered in Chapter 4. It is often accompanied by numerous physical complaints, such as headaches, muscle tension and gastrointestinal distress. For those with GAD, nearly every aspect of life invokes a thought of "what if" leading to a state of chronic worry. Not only do GAD sufferers worry all the time, but they also worry about their worries. Some even worry if they are *not* worrying. They may feel anxious about any number of things, including finances, school, work performance, airplane flights, personal safety, and the safety of loved ones. These anxieties and worries are often accompanied by a sense of "doom and gloom," a feeling that something bad is going to happen, despite evidence to the contrary.

Social phobia: Those with social phobia—also known as social anxiety disorder—suffer from an intense fear of doing or saying something that will embarrass them in a public or social setting. Fear of humiliation, rejection and separation may lead them to avoid situations where any of these fears might arise. This results in limiting activities only to those that are known, comfortable or predictable, and to avoiding any setting that is unfamiliar. This can manifest as a fear, whether of eating in public, attending parties, dating, taking exams, using a public restroom, and public speaking. (Fear of public speaking, in fact, is the number one fear, shared by an estimated 60 million people.)

It is important to note that these fears can affect many people, or even most people, to varying degrees. These disorders, by contrast, refer to manifestations of social anxiety that rise to levels of clinical significance. They are accompanied by marked impacts on personal, occupational and, in particular, social functioning, and they require pharmacologic and non-pharmacologic approaches to treatment.

Panic disorder: Panic is a brief, intense surge of anxiety, and a panic attack is a period of intense fear or excessive discomfort accompanied by a sensation of immediate danger in situations that may not actually be dangerous. Panic attacks can be debilitating. Symptom presentation may include shortness of breath, palpitations, dizziness, hot flashes or chills, a fear of losing control, even a fear of dying. Symptoms often come "out of the blue" and can occur in the absence of obvious stressors. They can even occur during sleep. Symptoms last anywhere from a few seconds to several minutes, but the residual effects can linger for several hours. Panic disorder is usually diagnosed when a person experiences at least four panic attacks in a month, or experiences at least one attack that is accompanied by the fear of another attack. In other words, people with panic disorder not only experience panic attacks, but also live continuously with the fear of having a panic attack.

Agoraphobia: The literal translation of agoraphobia is "fear of the marketplace," and historically, it has been associated with a fear of open spaces or public places. But today agoraphobia is believed to be a consequence or complication of panic disorder, particularly *untreated* panic attacks. In fact, approximately one in three people with panic disorder eventually develops agoraphobia, according to the Anxiety Disorders Association of America.

Those with agoraphobia fear experiencing a panic attack in a situation where escape may be difficult or embarrassing, or where it may be difficult to obtain help. These fears lead to the avoidance of many places, including automobiles, airplanes, elevators and crowded rooms. In extreme cases, people may stay in their homes for years, fearing that a panic attack would ensue if they were to venture outside their "safe zone."

Adjustment Disorder (AD): This disorder occurs in direct response to a specific event or other stressor. The DSM-IV TR lists the diagnostic criteria for AD as the development of emotional or behavioral symptoms in response to an identifiable stressor that occurs within three months of the onset of the stressor. Marked distress in excess of what would ordinarily be expected is present, as well as significant impairment in social or other functioning. Once the stressor ends, however, the symptoms do not persist for more than an additional six months. Examples include the termination of a relationship with a significant other, financial difficulties, and marital strife. Adjustment disorder is considered one of the sub-threshold disorders; as such, it is less well defined and can share characteristics of other diagnostic groups. Two common subtypes are adjustment disorder with depressed mood and adjustment disorder with anxiety.

Obsessive-Compulsive Disorder (OCD): In their book *Over and Over Again*, authors Fugen Neziroglu and Jose A. Yaryura-Tobias describe OCD as a "full-time companion." Though generally, it is not a cohort anyone would want to be around. Characterized by a series of persistent thoughts and compulsions, OCD is a chronic condition fraught with considerable suffering, shame, guilt and self-doubt. It is often incapacitating, as well.

While most people cling to some habits and routines in their daily lives, for those with OCD, the cycle of repetition can be nothing short of hell on earth. OCD is considered ego-dystonic, meaning most people want to either break or stop the patterns of obsessions and compulsions, but find they are unable to do so.

Obsessions are thoughts, images or even ideas that one continues to have over and over again. Common obsessions include a fear of contamination or "germophobia," safety concerns, a need for order or exactness, a fear of evil or sinful thoughts, a constant need for reassurance, and thinking repeatedly about certain words or numbers.

A compulsion, by contrast, is a ritualistic behavior or mental exercise performed in response to an obsession. Ostensibly, compulsions reduce the anxiety associated with the obsessions, but this relief is often short-lived. Common compulsions include:

- Washing and cleaning. For example, repeated washing of the hands or the floor.
- Checking. For example, repeated checking of door locks, window locks, electrical outlets or stove knobs.
- Ordering and arranging. For example, ordering table tops, writing instruments, clothes hangers or items in the refrigerator.
- Hoarding. For example, hoarding old newspapers and magazines, old clothes or canned goods.
- Mental exercises. For example, repeatedly counting to oneself, or silently stating the same phrase over and over.

As crippling as OCD can be on the individual experiencing it, the effect on their families may be devastating. OCD stirs family conflict, increases angst with regard as to how to "handle" or "manage life" with the affected individual, and fuels decisions that can lead to separations and divorces.

To say the least, the etiology of OCD has for years been controversial and sometimes baffling. The classic literature on OCD suggests the disorder is a psychological condition. But Judith L. Rapoport, M.D., of the National Institute of Mental Health, believes OCD may be a "disease of brain functioning." She has suggested that those with OCD have an increased metabolism in parts of the brain, namely, the prefrontal cortex and parts of the basal ganglia. This increase in metabolism, in turn, may trigger the emergence of primitive urges and behaviors that are OCD-like. (The pharmacological options available for treating OCD will be discussed in Chapter 10.)

Posttraumatic Stress Disorder (PTSD): This condition is brought on by surviving a severe or unusual mental or physical trauma. As the name suggests, issues surface *after* exposure to a real-life traumatic event in which the person believes he or she is in danger and feels extreme fear, horror or helplessness. Historically, PTSD has been considered a disorder most likely to affect soldiers who have been in combat. But in reality, PTSD affects twice as many women as men, according to a recent survey of more than 6,000 American adults.

For example, the lifetime prevalence rates of PTSD for Vietnam veterans and prisoners of war held in World War II are 31percent and 50 percent, respectively. But for rape victims, the range is 35 percent to 80 percent, according to *The Anxiety Answer Book* by Laurie A. Helgoe, Laura A. Wilhelm, and Martin J. Kommer. Other traumatic events may include childhood sexual or physical abuse, abortion, pregnancy loss, physical attack, being threatened with a weapon, cancer, abusive relationships, auto accidents, fire, and natural disasters such as tornadoes, earthquakes, hurricanes and floods.

Figure 9-3. How Do You Know It's PTSD?

- A sense of "flashback," feeling as if the initial trauma were happening all over again, with a sense of reliving the event
- Recurring nightmares or daydreams
- Avoiding people, places or things representative of the trauma, including conversations about the event
- Feelings of detachment or estrangement from others
- Intrusive, disturbing memories of the event
- Sleep disturbances
- Angry outbursts
- Hypervigilance, constantly "on guard"
- Disassociation with the event, feelings of "de-realization," a sense that the event did not actually happen

Specific Phobia: Specific phobias include the fear of dogs, cats, snakes and heights. They are generally not the focus of clinical attention. There is little reason to believe these phobias have a biological basis. As such, people rarely seek either behavioral or medication treatment to manage them.

Which of the anxiety disorders discussed above typically respond to medication management? What pharmacological choices are available, and how and when are they prescribed? Chapter 10 will address these questions and also examine other viable treatment alternatives.

10

MEDICATING ANXIETY

Patients who are being treated for anxiety disorders generally take medications known as anti-anxiety, or anxiolytic, drugs. These drugs are often prescribed in combination with psychotherapy, rendering the individual more susceptible to behavior-modification interventions. In addition, the antidepressants discussed in Chapter 5—tricyclics, monoamine oxidase inhibitors (MAOIs) and, in particular, the selective serotonin re-uptake inhibitors (SSRIs)—are also used in the treatment of some anxiety disorders, either in combination with a specific anti-anxiety drug or alone.

In this chapter, we will focus on the main classes of anti-anxiety drugs used to treat the most common anxiety disorders described in Chapter 9. Some of these medications are more effective than others for treating particular disorders, and some may need to be used in combination with SSRIs and other medications, especially in cases of Obsessive-Compulsive Disorder (OCD) and Post-Traumatic Stress Disorder (PTSD).

TYPES OF ANTI-ANXIETY DRUGS

Benzodiazepines: Benzodiazepines act throughout the central nervous system and have muscle relaxation, sedative, anxiolytic and anticonvulsant effects. As a class, they enhance the actions of GABA, which blocks the rapid release of stress hormones associated with anxiety and panic. Prescriber decisions as to which benzodiazepine to use are typically based on the anxiety disorder being treated, as well as on the onset of action and rate of elimination of the agent. For example, in the treatment of generalized anxiety disorder, longer half-life benzodiazepines, such as Valium (diazepam) and Klonopin (clonazepam), are often the drugs of choice, due to their longer duration of action.

Figure 10-1: Half-Lives of Benzodiazepines and Nonbenzodiazepines

The term "half-life" refers to the amount of time required for a medication to decrease its concentration by 50 percent relative to its peak level. Those with longer half-lives tend to be eliminated more slowly and therefore can build up in the system, whereas shorter half-life medications are more rapidly excreted leading to less system build up.

Half-life	Drug
6 hours or less	Lunesta* (eszopiclone), Halcion (triazolam), Sonata* (zaleplon), Ambien* (zolpidem), Ambien CR*(zolpidem CR), Rozerem* (ramelteon)
8 to 16 hours	Ativan (lorazepam), Restoril (temazepam), Xanax (alprazolam)
18 to 24 hours	Klonopin (clonazepam)
More than 24 hours	Valium (diazepam), Dalmane (flurazepam), Librium (chlordiazepoxide), Tranxene (clorazepate)

* Nonbenzodiazepine

In 1960, Librium (chlordiazepoxide) was the first benzodiazepine to reach the U.S. market. Three years later it was followed by Valium (diazepam). Today, benzodiazepines like Xanax (alprazolam) and Ativan (lorazepam) are frequently the drugs of choice for the treatment of panic disorders. That's because they work fast enough to manage the acute symptoms of panic—such as racing pulse and shortness of breath—yet long enough to control the residual anxiety symptoms that typically fuel the concern and worry about future attacks. Benzodiazepines are often used in conjunction with SSRI antidepressants in the treatment of panic. Benzodiazepines, when used short term, can be particularly effective in managing adjustment disorders with anxious mood, such as a recent job loss, death of a close friend or family member, or recent divorce.

With regard to OCD, benzodiazepines generally do not possess anti-obsessional properties. Instead, the serotonin antidepressants—such as Prozac (fluoxetine), Zoloft (sertraline), Paxil (paroxetine), Anafranil (clomipramine) and Luvox (fluvoxamine)—are preferentially the first-line agents in the treatment of OCD. The inhibitory effects of serotonin help reduce the incidences of primitive urges which are OCD-like. They are effective in about half of all patients.

OCD is typically treated with higher doses of serotonin antidepressants—as much as two to three times higher than those used to treat depression and other anxiety disorders. Response to medication typically occurs slowly over a period of eight to 12 weeks. In both non- and partial-responders to SSRIs, atypical antipsychotics (discussed in Chapter 3) are considered viable augmenting agents. Also, cognitive-behavioral therapy—particularly in-vivo response and prevention techniques—is a vital component of OCD treatment and should be considered for *all* of those who either don't respond or only partially respond to SSRIs. Regardless of the treatment modalities employed, however, complete symptom remission is rarely if ever attainable. OCD is unfortunately a chronic "disorder of repetition" with a waxing and waning long-term symptom course.

Benzodiazepines may be effective in managing some of the associated Axis I clinical symptoms of PTSD, such as panic attacks and hyperarousal. They are often combined with the SSRIs to enhance symptom control and management. Also, the atypical antipsychotic Seroquel (quetiapine) (discussed in Chapter 3) and the anti-hypertensive medication Minipress (prazosin) have shown promise in reducing and "deconsolidating" traumatic nightmares associated with PTSD. Psychotherapy, in conjunction with medication management, is almost always warranted to help patients deal with the often profound effects of having experienced a trauma.

While benzodiazepines are popular and widely used, they are not without problems. Mainly, the risk of dependence can be significant. For this reason, prescribers should use caution when keeping patients on benzodiazepines for extended periods of time. Some clinicians prescribe them for only days or weeks; others prescribe them for six months and longer. Also, benzodiazepines can be dangerous in overdose, particularly when combined with alcohol. Because of their potential for dependency and abuse, benzodiazepines need to be closely monitored. When discontinued, their dosage must be decreased slowly over days, weeks or even months to prevent withdrawal symptoms, which are similar in presentation to the symptoms of anxiety.

Non-benzodiazepines: If you believe the news reports, Americans are in the midst of a sleep-deprivation crisis. Television commercials show everything from luna moths entering an open bedroom window to Abe Lincoln and a groundhog reassuring a weary insomniac that his "dreams miss him," and that his sleep problems are treatable.

One estimate puts the cost of sleep deprivation to U.S. businesses at $150 billion a year in absenteeism and lost productivity. There may be something to it. In a recent University of Pennsylvania study, subjects who slept only four to six hours a night for 14 consecutive nights displayed significant deficits in cognitive performance, equivalent to going without sleep for up to three days in a row. Indeed, roughly one in four Americans use some form of sleeping pill or other aid, and according to BioMarket, a biotech research company, in 2004 Americans spent $2 billion on Ambien (zolpidem) alone.

Non-benzodiazepines such as Ambien (zolpidem), Sonata (zaleplon) and Lunesta (eszopiclone) are often utilized in the treatment of primary insomnia. Some studies suggest that these agents are associated with less dependence and less cognitive impairment than the benzodiazepines. Historically, benzodiazepines degrade sleep quality over time, leading many users to conclude that their insomnia worsens the longer they use them. These non-benzodiazepines, however, have demonstrated less of a propensity for interfering with rapid eye movement (REM) sleep as well as Stage III and IV delta sleep, two of the primary components of "sleep architecture." Therefore, they are preferentially utilized in the management of insomnia.

Sepracor, the manufacturer of Lunesta (eszopiclone), claims that the drug produces a total sleep time of seven hours, compared with five hours with Ambien (zolpidem), and that the onset to sleep is approximately 10 minutes. In fact, one of my patients recently commented on the importance of "already being in bed" before taking Lunesta (eszopiclone). This drug is also FDA-approved for regular use for periods of up to six months. By comparison, Ambien (zolpidem) and Sonata (zaleplon) are FDA-approved for only as much as two weeks of use. The new Ambien CR (zolpidem CR), a competitor to Lunesta (eszopiclone), is an extended-release formulation that is FDA-approved for both sleep induction and maintenance.

In 2007, a large National Institute of Health sponsored study concluded that sleeping medication will reduce sleep latency (the time it takes to go from full wakefulness to falling asleep) by about 30 minutes, and that total sleep time will be increased by only 11 minutes. Several studies have indicated that cognitive behavioral therapy is just as effective as medication and has a more lasting overall benefit.

The side effects of the non-benzodiazepines are similar to those of the previously discussed benzodiazepines. But Ambien (zolpidem) has been linked to reports of sleepwalking, sleep-eating and sleep-driving behaviors in some users. Recent literature reports indicate that Ambien (zolpidem) may interfere in some way with the sleep-wake cycle; after taking this medication, some users engage in these physical behaviors with no recollection of having done so. The FDA has issued warnings regarding the possibility of this effect in susceptible individuals.

Rozerem (ramelteon), a relatively new prescription sleep aid, is a non-controlled substance, unlike the benzodiazepines and non-benzodiazepines. As such, the drug is not linked to abuse or dependence. Rozerem (ramelteon) is "melatonin-like" in that it targets two specific melatonin receptor sites in the brain, thereby contributing to its sleep-promoting properties. Melatonin is believed to be involved in the maintenance of the circadian rhythm associated with the sleep-wake cycle. Reported common side effects of Rozerem (rameteon) are drowsiness, fatigue and dizziness.

Another non-benzodiazepine, BuSpar (buspirone), is approved only for the treatment of GAD (generalized anxiety disorder). Advantages of Buspar (buspirone) over the benzodiazepines include little, if any, sedation, no development of tolerance or dependence, and no potentiation effect if used with alcohol. Disadvantages include a slow onset of action and a lack of efficacy, particularly in prior benzodiazepine users. The drug does not have a major effect on the GABA system, but instead exerts its effects on the serotonin system. This is a likely explanation for its relative slowness in taking effect. Side effects are typically minimal and include dizziness, headache, nausea, nervousness and agitation.

Antihistamines: This drug class is used primarily to counteract the effects of histamine, a body chemical involved in allergic reactions. But they also can reduce anxiety through their sedative effects and are sometimes used to treat insomnia. (If you've ever taken a Benadryl (diphenhydramine), you know what I mean!) Although not FDA-approved for insomnia, antihistamines can help a patient fall asleep; however, they will not help the patient stay asleep, nor will they prevent early morning awakenings, the other two markers of insomnia. Antihistamine use may produce a hangover effect or residual grogginess.

Vistaril (hydroxyzine pamoate) and Atarax (hydroxyzine hydrochloride) are two prescription antihistamines that are used to treat insomnia and symptoms of anxiety, nervous tension and allergies. Unlike the benzodiazepines, antihistamines are not associated with a risk of dependency. Possible side effects include nausea, fatigue, sedation and dizziness.

Beta-blockers: These drugs, including Inderal (propranolol) and Tenormin (atenolol), have been used in general medicine since 1965. By blocking beta- receptors in the heart, blood pressure, heart rate and cardiac output are decreased. This has led to clinical uses in the treatment of hypertension, angina and cardiac arrhythmias. In psychiatry, beta-blockers are used in the treatment of anxiety disorders with manifestations such as palpitations, sweating and tremor. Performance anxiety that may affect public speakers, musicians or those taking an examination seem to be well suited for beta-blocker treatment. These medications may be taken as needed approximately one to two hours prior to a stressful event. When use is carefully monitored, side effects are generally mild and include weakness, tiredness and possibly bradycardia (slowed heart rate). Beta-blockers are contraindicated in patients with asthma, emphysema and other respiratory diseases. Incidental use of Inderal (propranolol) in performance anxiety is usually in a dosage range of 10 mg to 60 mg, one to two hours prior to the stress-related event.

Catapres (clonidine): Also an effective antihypertensive agent, the usefulness of Catapres (clonidine) in the treatment of anxiety is related to its effectiveness in easing some of the peripheral symptoms associated with opiate and alcohol withdrawal, such as tremulousness, profuse sweating, motor restlessness, anxiety and agitation. It can also ease insomnia, due to its sedative effects.

WHAT YOU AND YOUR CLIENTS NEED TO KNOW

Probably the greatest concern for patients with regard to the use of antianxiety medications is the potential for physical and/or psychological dependence. This is particularly important with the use of benzodiazepines, which pose the greatest risk due to the "quick fix" aspect of their action. While most patients do not abuse benzodiazepines, the temptation to increase the dosage—or, worse, to add alcohol to the mix—is real and serious. This and other side effects should be monitored closely by prescribers and associated treating professionals.

Figure 10-2. Side Effects of Antianxiety Agents

Antianxiety Agent	Side Effects
Benzodiazepines Examples: Valium (diazepam), Librium (chlordiazepoxide), Xanax (alprazolam) and Ativan (lorazepam), Klonopin (clonazepam)	Drowsiness, possible confusion, dizziness, imbalance, potential for physical and psychological dependence. If taken with alcohol, extreme drowsiness and even respiratory depression can occur. Signs of possible overdose include slurred speech and memory problems.
Nonbenzodiazepines Examples: Ambien (zolpidem), Sonata (zaleplon), Lunesta (eszopiclone)	Drowsiness, dizziness, fatigue, sleepwalking, possible interference with REM sleep and sleep/wake cycling. Potential for dependence, withdrawal and tolerance.
Rozerem (ramelteon)	Drowsiness, dizziness, nausea, fatigue, headache, and insomnia. No risk of dependence.
BuSpar (buspirone)	Headache, nausea, dizziness and possible adverse effects on patients with liver or kidney disease. No risk of dependence. No potentiation with alcohol.

Antihistamines Examples: Benadryl (diphenhydramine), Vistaril (hydroxyzine pamoate), Atarax (hydroxyzine hydrochloride)	Drowsiness, fatigue, dry mouth, twitches, tremors.
Beta blockers Examples: Inderal (propranolol), Tenormin (atenolol)	Depression, fatigue, drowsiness, dizziness, lightheadedness, bradycardia (slow heart rate), hypotension (lowered blood pressure). Contraindicated in cases of asthma and emphysema.
Catapres (clonidine)	Dizziness, drowsiness, postural hypotension (drop in blood pressure when rising quickly from a sitting or lying position), bradycardia (slow heart rate), dry mouth.

CASE STUDY: PANIC DISORDER—"ELEVATOR TO THE 52ND FLOOR"

Philip is a 33-year-old attorney who recently became a full partner in his small law firm. He is married and is the father of two children, ages 3 and 5. He self-referred to you, a Licensed Clinical Social Worker, on the recommendation of a friend you treated two years ago. When you ask Philip why he has decided to see you, he states that two days ago, he and three of his fellow attorneys left their office for a routine business lunch. Upon returning, they boarded the elevator to their office on the 52nd floor. Philip says the elevator moved very slowly, eventually coming to a complete stop between the 51st and 52nd floors. Not overly concerned by this, he was able to call the building maintenance department and alert them of their predicament. Although the maintenance department worked diligently to get the elevator moving again, their attempts were in vain. Philip and his colleagues were trapped in the elevator for more than five hours. They were eventually "welded out" through the elevator's top panel and pulled to safety along the cable structure. Philip stated that although the situation was harrowing, at no point did he "fall apart" or fear for his life.

However, since that incident, Philip reports that he has been unable to board any elevator. Upon approaching one, he becomes shaky, lightheaded and short of breath, and he starts to tremble. Philip reports no previous personal or family psychiatric history. His colleagues have allowed him to work from home for now, provided that he seeks treatment.

Diagnostic Considerations

While conducting a thorough assessment of Philip's presenting problem, you ask when he had last seen his primary care physician for a routine physical examination. Philip replies that he visited his physician approximately two months prior to the elevator incident, and that he was found to be in good health. He also explains that he has no personal or family history of psychiatric illness or substance abuse. The discussion now centers on his harrowing circumstances with the elevator. You mention that although via self-report he had not panicked during the incident itself, he has developed anticipatory anxiety and has become phobic of elevator use. You explain that if these symptoms remained unchecked, panic attacks may emerge. As such, you suggest a psychiatric referral. Philip readily consents.

Treatment Course

The consulting psychiatrist decides to start Philip on Xanax (alprazolam) at 0.25 mg three times daily for management of the associated anxiety. After one week, with Philip's consent, Celexa (citalopram) at 20 mg daily is added to the treatment regimen. After three weeks, Philip reports feeling markedly less anxious, and the psychiatrist discontinues the Xanax (alprazolam) use, while increasing the Celexa (citalopram) dose to 40 mg daily. As this point, Philip consents to do cognitive-behavioral work. This involves systematic desensitization techniques accompanied by measured exposure to help Philip overcome his elevator phobia. After four months of behavioral work, together with the Celexa (citalopram) use, Philip is consistently able to board and ride the building's elevators up to his 52nd floor office without major incident.

CASE STUDY: OCD "I WANT TO STOP ACTING SO WEIRD."

Douglas is a 46-year-old model maker for a high-tech Fortune 500 company. He was referred to you, a Licensed Professional Counselor, by his parish priest, whom Douglas consulted with for help with anxiety and "behavioral repetition." Douglas tells you that over the last six months, he has found it increasingly difficult to "get out of the house." Douglas mentions that although he has always been a "safety freak" of sorts, some of his recent behavior has been extreme. In recent days, for example, he has returned home as many as 15 times after leaving for work. Each time, he checks the locks on all of the doors and windows, makes sure the appliances are unplugged, and ensures that no water is running from any of the faucets. He also mentions a desire for "order" at his office workspace and says that when a fellow worker stops by and touches or moves something on his desk, Douglas feels annoyed.

In obvious distress, Douglas shares that he feels shame, guilt and increasing self-doubt about all of this. He wants to stop acting "so weird." He also reveals that just last week, his wife asked Douglas for a divorce, saying she could no longer tolerate his "very strange tendencies." Douglas also fears that he is about to be fired from his job.

Douglas further reports that his father, a pharmacist, essentially had to retire "in shame" from his work in a retail pharmacy several years ago. The father would repeatedly check the contents of prescription bottles and labels to such an extent that customers complained vehemently about having to wait too long.

Diagnostic Considerations

Having completed your initial assessment, you decide to commend Douglas for having the courage to address these concerns. You inquire about his understanding of OCD and its associated symptoms. He states that he knows little about it, outside of a recent discussion he had listened to on a daytime TV talk show. For explanatory purposes, and to put Douglas at ease, you mention that the disorder has received increasingly more attention over the last few years, that it is considered genetic, and that it is best treated through a combination of medication and behavioral therapies. Douglas consents to begin seeing a psychiatrist colleague of yours who specializes in OCD and has conducted numerous medication clinical trials regarding its management.

Treatment Course

Douglas is started on Paxil (paroxetine) 20 mg daily for one week. In the second week of treatment, the dose is increased to 40 mg daily, and by week three, to 60 mg per day. Throughout the dosage increases, Douglas complains of troubling side effects, including dry mouth, sweating, constipation, and an increasing lack of motivation that he finds particularly troubling. The psychiatrist explains to Douglas that these side effects are consistent with dosage increases, and he recommends ways to best manage them.

Douglas begins to show some initial symptom improvement after six weeks of Paxil (paroxetine) use. But after taking Paxil (paroxetine) at 60 mg per day for three months, Douglas's symptom improvement has essentially plateaued. The atypical antipsychotic Risperdal (risperidone), at a dose of 4 mg per day, is added to the Paxil, and Douglas was instructed to remain on this regimen for another nine months.

From the outset of treatment, you employed a series of "in-vivo response and prevention" cognitive-behavioral techniques to augment medication management. Douglas's symptoms waxed and waned over one year of treatment. Before he leaves treatment, you explain to him that OCD is a chronic disorder for which there is no "cure." Therefore, symptoms tend not to completely remit, but only gradually improve.

CASE STUDY: PTSD—"WATER, WATER EVERYWHERE: A PERSONAL STORY"

On August 29, 2005, Hurricane Katrina made landfall in Louisiana. The storm completely engulfed the state's coastal parishes before plowing into the greater New Orleans area. In its wake, Katrina left catastrophic damage. More than 150,000 homes and thousands of lives succumbed to the floodwaters, which consumed 85 percent of the city. The day before, I evacuated New Orleans, making my way by automobile to Oxford, Mississippi. A typical five-hour drive mushroomed into a 13-hour ordeal. I checked into a Days Inn where I had secured a reservation for three days. As it became painfully clear I would not be able to return to New Orleans, that initial three-day stay turned into a nine-day stay. I was then asked to leave so that the hotel could honor another reservation.

Dazed, numb and confused, I decided to head for Conroe, Texas, where I had friends. I spent a few days with them before settling into a room at a nearby Holiday Inn Express. With little to occupy my time, I found myself utterly mesmerized by what was happening in New Orleans. After a couple of days of remaining glued to the 24-hour TV news channels, I began experiencing recurring nightmares of what I had seen unfolding before my eyes on television. I had images of floodwaters rising in the street in front of my home, rushing past my porch and entering my house with a fury. This went on for several days and was accompanied by feelings of extreme vulnerability, hypervigilance and insomnia. Then came denial, as I attempted to convince myself that the railroad tracks that parallel my street had buffered my home from the rising water. Reality finally set in, though, as I had acquired enough evidence that my home had not been spared. Emotional numbness, feelings of emptiness and very poor concentration followed.

I returned to New Orleans several weeks aster to stay with a dear friend. That stay lasted an entire year. Soon after my return, I decided it was in my best interest to seek treatment. After a thorough medical, psychological and psychosocial workup and assessment, the treating clinician diagnosed posttraumatic stress disorder (PTSD), acute onset. Then a host of cognitive-behavioral therapies ensued, including EMDR (eye movement desensitization and reprocessing), but no medication. I remained in weekly treatment for three months and have followed up with occasional visits as needed. Overall, the treatment was quite successful. From time to time, though, I feel a sense of longing for the old neighborhood where I was raised and spent my entire life. Nonetheless, I have decided to stay in New Orleans and have purchased another house in the area—this time, on much "higher ground."

DOSAGE RANGE CHART — ANTI-ANXIETY MEDICATIONS, SLEEP AGENTS

BRAND NAME	GENERIC NAME	CLASS	DAILY DOSAGE RANGE *
Ambien	zolpidem	nonbenzodiazepine	5 mg – 10 mg
Ativan	lorazepam	benzodiazepine	2 mg – 6 mg
BuSpar	buspirone	nonbenzodiazepine	15 mg – 60 mg
Klonopin	clonazepam	benzodiazepine	0.5 mg – 4 mg
Lunesta	eszopiclone	nonbenzodiazepine	1 mg – 3 mg
Rozerem	ramelteon	melatonin type	8 mg
Sonata	zaleplon	nonbenzodiazepine	5 mg – 10 mg
Valium	diazepam	benzodiazepine	5 mg – 40mg
Xanax	alprazolam	benzodiazepine	0.5 mg – 4 mg

* Suggested adult dose

Note: Dosage ranges may vary depending on source, and may also vary according to age.

11

EXPECTANT MOTHERS, THE YOUNG, AND THE CHALLENGES OF FATHER TIME

PREGNANCY

Physicians have been understandably reluctant to prescribe psychotropic medications to women who are either pregnant or contemplating pregnancy. For one, there's the paucity of reliable data associated with their use. For another, there are unknown risks to the fetus. Also, few women would intentionally place their unborn children at possible risk by using psychiatric medications while pregnant.

However, nearly half of all pregnancies are unplanned, and significant numbers of women of childbearing age are taking medications for anxiety, depression, schizophrenia, bipolar disorder and other psychiatric conditions. This means that a considerable number of women are becoming pregnant at the same time they are being treated for a mental illness. This population must be informed, to the degree possible, of the risks of taking these drugs during pregnancy and nursing.

Despite the lack of extensive data, evidence-based information from epidemiologic studies indicates that most psychotropic drugs are relatively safe during pregnancy. Also, there is also another issue to consider: Not treating pregnant women with a psychiatric diagnosis may be far riskier than the possible drawbacks and complications to the woman or child if psychotropic medications were employed during pregnancy. For example, stopping medications in a woman with a serious illness, such as schizophrenia or bipolar disorder, could trigger a relapse that might endanger both the woman and her baby (poor self care, inadequate nutrition, poor prenatal and antenatal care). Still, it's normal for expectant mothers and physicians alike to be apprehensive about the use of psychiatric medications during pregnancy. The most important indicator of a healthy baby is a healthy mother.

Because safety issues for both mother and child are of paramount importance, the important risk factors linked to drug use during pregnancy should be addressed. The major one is teratogenesis, or birth defects involving the malformation of the fetus or fetal organs. Teratogenesis is often a result of neural tube defects, in which the brain and spinal cord fail to fuse together properly. Spina bifida, or "cleft spine," is a common example. Two other teratogenic manifestations are facial deformity and cleft palate. Drugs that produce these malformations are known as teratogens.

There is also a behavioral teratogenesis—defined as the long-term effects on the child resulting from drug exposure *in utero*. These effects can manifest as learning difficulties and developmental delays. Also, more information has surfaced on the subject of poor neonatal adaptation, meaning the residual effects on the newborn that can include such symptoms as hypothermia (low body temperature), difficulties in eating and sleeping, tachycardia (rapid heartbeat) and irritability.

Antidepressants: According to recent data, none of the antidepressants that have been studied in pregnancy have been found to increase the baseline rate of 1 percent to 3 percent for major malformations. Some studies, however, report an increased rate of spontaneous abortions. The SSRIs as well as most of the cyclics are not associated with teratogenesis. In December of 2005 however, the FDA issued a public health advisory regarding first trimester exposure to Paxil (paroxetine) and cardiac malformations (1.5-2 percent vs. non-exposed 1 percent). During 2006, reports indicated that as many as 30 percent of children with third trimester exposure to SSRIs showed withdrawal: lack of crying, increased muscle tone, irritability and poor sleep.

The MAOIs—Remeron (mirtazapine), Effexor (venlafaxine) and Wellbutrin (bupropion)—have not been studied extensively. Antidepressants are present in breast milk; therefore, nursing is contraindicated for women taking these drugs.

Lithium is generally not recommended during pregnancy. Its use has been linked to neonatal effects, including impaired respiration and EKG and heart-rate abnormalities. Exposure in the first trimester is strongly associated with fetal cardiac irregularities. Lithium is also linked to Ebstein's Anomaly, a heart defect in which the tricuspid valve malfunctions. Lithium is highly concentrated in breast milk; therefore, nursing is contraindicated for women taking this drug.

<u>Antipsychotics</u>: There is no evidence showing that conventional antipsychotics increase the rates of major malformations. Establishing the lowest possible effective dose certainly makes sense, since there has been some evidence of short-term neonatal motor activity. There is little information on the safety of the newer, atypical antipsychotics. All of the antipsychotics are excreted in breast milk.

<u>Benzodiazepines</u>: Although there is insufficient evidence to prove that benzodiazepines are teratogens, many believe that the use of this class of drugs should be avoided during the first trimester of pregnancy, due to a risk of oral cleft. A significant concern with benzodiazepine use during pregnancy is the emergence of neonatal CNS depression and withdrawal symptoms. Other symptoms of abrupt discontinuation syndrome include sedation, hypotonia (loss of muscle tonicity), apnea, reluctance to suck and cyanosis. Benzodiazepines are secreted in breast milk and can cause sedation and slowed heart rate.

<u>Anticonvulsants:</u> Tegretol (carbamazepine) and Depakote (divalproex sodium) are established human teratogens. They should both be avoided during pregnancy. Also, both are present in breast milk. These drugs are also linked to long-term neurodevelopmental effects on offspring well into adolescence, such as EEG pattern changes, expressive language and developmental delays, and intellectual performance. Information on the newer anticonvulsants that has recently come to light is more promising. Specifically, Lamictal (lamotrigine), Trileptal (oxcarbazepine) and Neurontin (gabapentin), when used during pregnancy, do not increase the risk of major birth malformations.

OLDER ADULTS

Safe medication use in an aging population requires vigilance. Patients and their caregivers must keep track of the quantity and type of medications, make sure they are taken properly and regularly, and watch for any adverse side effects and interactions. These challenges are related to the very real physiological factors that clinicians must face when prescribing and administering medications to older adults.

Dosing concerns arise with the elderly. Body weights change, metabolism slows and stomachs do not absorb substances as well as they once did. Kidneys and livers don't process fluids and toxins as efficiently—there can be as much as a 40 percent reduction in the clearance of certain drugs. "Start low and go slow" can be a helpful rule of thumb when prescribing to an aging population that is often more sensitive to the effects of medication. In post-menopausal women in particular, fatty tissue increases, which can raise the concentrations of certain drugs. Older people also tend to have proportionally less body water, so blood levels of a water-soluble drug can also be higher than would be expected. These physiological changes affect both the pharmacokinetics and pharmacodynamics that were examined in Chapter 1.

Also, the elderly generally take more medications, and tend to "self-medicate" with over-the-counter drugs and herbal supplements, more than younger adults. This increases the possibility of drug interactions. Some estimates place the incidence of drug interactions at 6 percent in patients taking two medications a day—and as high as 50 percent in those taking five a day.

OLDER ADULTS: WHAT YOU NEED TO KNOW

Prescribers and non-prescribers will likely be seeing more elderly patients as the oldest of the "baby boomers" approach retirement. In the United States, people aged 65 and over make up just 13 percent of the total population, but account for 30 percent of all prescriptions written.

Changes in mental status can be drug-related. Benzodiazepines can cause drowsines, confusion, prolonged sedation and memory loss. Cyclic antidepressants like Elavil (amitriptyline) can cause confusion, and even delirium, when used in the elderly. Benzodiazepines and cyclic antidepressants have historically been linked to falls and various types of fractures.

Watch for signs of noncompliance. It sometimes takes longer to see a therapeutic effect with psychotropic medications used in seniors, placing them at risk for abruptly discontinuing their medications due to slowed response rates. Advancing age is often accompanied by less patience. Older adults should be encouraged to continue to take their medications unless otherwise instructed by their physician or other prescriber.

Memory often declines with age, too. Encourage patients to keep an updated list of medications with them at all times. Provide a copy of this list to a family member.

Elderly patients may be getting their prescriptions from more than one pharmacy. Encourage them to use only one source for the purchase of *all* medications—prescription and over-the-counter. Pharmacies now have computer software that can check for potentially problematic drug interactions.

Watch for additional medications prescribed to alleviate the side effects of an already prescribed one. For example, a sleep aid may be prescribed to offset the side effect of insomnia from an antidepressant. This can set up a vicious cycle of polypharmacy, a growing and potentially serious concern in the elderly.

CHILDREN AND ADOLESCENTS

We now know that age is not a factor in psychiatric disorders. This wasn't always the case. Twenty years ago, clinical communities didn't even believe mood disorders were diagnosable in children. There was a veritable absence of data supporting medication use in children. We have since learned that mood disorders, such as major depression and bipolar disorder, are unquestionably diagnosable in children and adolescents. As a result, psychotropic medication use by children for the treatment of mood disorders has tripled in the last 10 years. There is still, however, a paucity of reliable data addressing psychopharmacology in children and adolescents (ADD/ADHD excluded).

Important points to remember with regard to child psychopharmacology include:

- Some medications are more rapidly metabolized by children and have greater renal clearance, generally up to puberty.
- More rapid metabolism in children may sometimes require dosing that is equal to or even greater than doses used by adults.
- The variability in responses to psychotropic medication are likely due, at least in part, to neurotransmitter systems are not fully developed. In fact, according to some research reports, these systems sometimes do not fully develop until age 21 or 22.

CHILDREN AND MOOD DISORDERS

Depression: According to the National Mental Health Association, one in three American children—some of pre-school age—suffer from depression. Because children and adolescents tend not to spontaneously report symptoms, we often need to rely on observations from parents or primary caretakers.

Signs and symptoms of pediatric depression include:

- Persistent sadness
- Lack of energy, motivation or enthusiasm
- Changes in sleep or eating patterns (too much or too little)
- Irritability, agitation and unwarranted crying
- In toddlers, developmental delays in language or walking.
- Inappropriate, sad or morbid play that concentrates on harming themselves or others
- Boredom and failure at school

According to the NIMH, approximately one in 20 teens has moderately severe to severe major depression, making major depression one of the most common disorders of adolescence. It occurs in both boys and girls. A substantial number have suicidal thoughts. Without effective treatment, some will eventually commit suicide.

MEDICATING DEPRESSION IN CHILDREN AND ADOLESCENTS

Cyclic antidepressants have been used for years in young people. The FDA has approved their use for children at least 12 years old. The prototype cyclic antidepressant has historically been Tofranil (imipramine). It has been prescribed for the treatment of Attention Deficit Hyperactivity Disorder (ADHD), school-phobia, night terrors, sleepwalking disorder and enuresis (bedwetting). However, as discussed in Chapter 5, the cyclic antidepressants are extremely dangerous in overdose and are fraught with potentially serious side effects. For example, six cases of sudden death have been reported in children using Norpramin (desipramine) due to suspected cardiac arrhythmias.

The selective serotonin reuptake inhibitors (SSRIs) are today considered first-line agents of choice for the treatment of pediatric depression. Although the clinical studies are sparse, they show that SSRIs are better tolerated and more effective than the cyclics.

Since 2004, *all* antidepressants on the U.S. drug market have carried an FDA "black box" warning on the package. This label states that there is a possible risk of suicide when used by children and adolescents. We are left with a considerable amount of uncertainty regarding the use of antidepressants, especially in young people under 18. There seems to be evidence that suicidal ideation may emerge during the early phases of treatment with antidepressants. There is no evidence though that this increases the risk of completed suicide. (No suicides in 4000+ children in any of these studies).

BIPOLAR DISORDER

An article in the September 2007 issue of the *Archives of General Psychiatry* provided strong evidence that the diagnosis of bipolar disorder is rising, especially in children. Office visits by children diagnosed with bipolar disorder increased significantly during the 10-year period of 1994 to 2003. Disagreements abound as to what this means. Some view it as progress, in that a disorder that has long gone undiagnosed in this population group is now being better screened and treated. Some of the clinical literature suggests that bipolar symptoms may emerge as early as infancy. Others, however, are more skeptical and perceive it as gross overdiagnosis.

The truth is that bipolar disorder is quite difficult to accurately diagnose in children. Many of its characteristic symptoms overlap with other disorders, particularly ADHD. Also, in contrast to adults, children and adolescents in the manic phase of the disorder tend toward extreme irritability and destructive outbursts, as opposed to the euphoria more common to adults. The depressed phase is often characterized by physical aches and pains, social isolation, hypersensitivity to rejection, frequent absences from school, and talk of running away from home. Also, daily mood cycling is more common in children than in adults.

Not surprisingly, there is also limited data on medications used to treat bipolar disorder in this population. Most typically, Lithobid or other brand lithium, or the mood stabilizing anticonvulsants such as Depakote (divalproex), Lamictal (lamotrigine) and Trileptal (oxcarbazepine), are utilized in children and adolescents. Studies are also investigating various forms of psychotherapy for young people in combination with medications.

ANXIETY DISORDERS

According to the National Mental Health Information Center, anxiety disorders are among the most common mental, emotional and behavioral problems to occur during childhood and adolescence. About 13 out of every 100 children and adolescents ages 9 to 17 experience some kind of anxiety disorder; girls are affected more than boys. If left untreated, these disorders can lead to the inability to finish school, impaired social relations, low self-esteem, and eventually, anxiety disorders in adulthood.

The onset of childhood anxiety usually begins between the ages of six and eight. Children at this age typically become less afraid of the dark and other imaginary dangers, and they become more afraid and anxious about performance in school and interactions with friends.

Some studies suggest that anxiety disorders in children are heritable, particularly from parents that have met anxiety disorder criteria themselves. But there is no way to prove whether the disorders are a result of biology, the environment, or both.

Below is a brief description of several types of anxiety disorders diagnosable in children and adolescents:

Overanxious disorder of childhood: This is similar to adult generalized anxiety disorder (GAD). Children and adolescents with this disorder engage in unrealistic and extreme worry about almost everything—their academic performance, athletic capability, even punctuality. Tense, self-conscious and having a strong desire for reassurance, these young people may complain about aches and pains that have no physical cause.

Panic disorder: In children and young teenagers, panic is rare. Rates begin to rise in older adolescents, particularly girls. As they can for adults, repeated panic attacks can be a sign of panic disorder. These attacks may be accompanied by symptoms that include a pounding heartbeat, dizziness, nausea, and feelings of imminent harm or death, accompanied by intense fear.

Obsessive-compulsive disorder (OCD): Like OCD adults, children and adolescents with OCD become trapped in patterns of repetitive thoughts and actions that are difficult to stop. These actions may include repeated hand washing, counting, hair pulling, nail biting, repetitive questioning, arranging and rearranging objects, and a strong need to control others and their environment. Children and adolescents often have much higher rates of aggressive obsessions, such as thoughts of harming themselves or others, and sexual acting out. Childhood and adolescent OCD is highly co-morbid with mood, anxiety, tic and disruptive behavior disorders.

The National Institute of Mental Health (NIMH) suggests that nearly 10 percent of adult OCD sufferers have had symptoms since the ages of five to 10. More than 20 percent have had them by ages 10 to 15. And more than 40 percent had them by ages 15 to 20. In all, approximately 2 percent of the general population of children and adolescents meet OCD criteria.

Separation anxiety disorder: Most often, this disorder manifests as school phobia, not wanting to attend camp, or even stay at a friend's house for fear of leaving their parents. These children are frequently described as "clingy." This disorder can be accompanied by sadness, withdrawal or a baseless fear of losing a family member to death or other permanent separation.

PTSD. The symptoms of post-traumatic stress disorder in children are similar to those in adults, with the addition of manifestations such as "monster nightmares," and re-enacting a stressful event through play. Children and adolescents can develop PTSD after experiencing physical or sexual abuse; being a victim of or witnessing violence; and living through a natural or manmade disaster (hurricane, bombing, etc.). In young children, domestic violence is the most common cause of PTSD.

MEDICATION MANAGEMENT OF PEDIATRIC ANXIETY DISORDERS

Studies on the medication management of anxiety disorders in youth are sparse and inconclusive, and there are few specific guidelines for treating them. While benzodiazepines are used to treat anxiety and sleeplessness in children, the data supporting their use are minimal. While some anecdotal evidence has suggested possible benefit from Buspar (buspirone) in children, this continues to be unproven. Antihistamines such as Benadryl (diphenhydramine) and Vistaril (hydroxyzine) have been used for decades to ameliorate anxiety symptoms in psychiatrically disturbed children. Anafranil (clomipramine), Luvox (fluvoxamine) and Zoloft (sertraline) have FDA indications for children and adolescents with OCD. Experience with the SSRIs in controlled pediatric studies has led clinicians to consider these agents for treating non-OCD anxiety disorders as well. Controlled studies and supportive data are significantly lacking in the treatment of pediatric anxiety disorders with the beta-blockers.

Cognitive-behavioral interventions have proven to be effective for a majority of children and adolescents with anxiety disorders. Between 50 percent to 80 percent, after these non-pharmacological interventions, no longer met anxiety disorder diagnostic criteria.

PSYCHOTIC DISORDERS

As discussed in Chapter 2, psychotic disorders can involve an extreme impairment in the ability to distinguish reality from fantasy, behave in an emotionally appropriate manner, and communicate effectively. The National Institutes of Health (NIH) indicates that schizophrenia is rare in children: Only about one in 1,000 have this disorder. Adolescent onset generally occurs between the ages of 11 and 15. Young people who do suffer from schizophrenia have psychotic periods that can involve hallucinations, social isolation, loss of contact with reality, anhedonia (inability to experience pleasure) and delusional thoughts.

The latest research indicates that for the first time, the gene implicated in schizophrenia in adults has also been linked to schizophrenia in children. In June 2007, the NIMH and the NIH convened a meeting for discussion among basic, translational, and clinical investigators to review the current knowledge on causes, neurobiology, developmental trajectory, and treatment of child and adolescent onset schizophrenia. The scientific workshop focused on three important areas: opportunities for expanding current knowledge of causes and neurobiology of child and adolescent onset schizophrenia; critical next steps to translate current understanding of behavioral/cognitive characteristics and underlying neurobiology into treatment development; and current challenges to conducting research in this area, and strategies to overcome them.

MEDICATION MANAGEMENT OF CHILD AND ADOLESCENT PSYCHOTIC DISORDERS

The drugs of choice in the treatment of psychotic disorders in children and adolescents, regardless of the presentation, are the atypical antipsychotics. In 2007, Risperdal (risperidone) and Abilify (aripiprazole) gained approval for the treatment of schizophrenia in adolescents ages 13 to 17. Research is still in its infancy with respect to the treatment of the stereotypical symptoms of the pervasive developmental disorders Autism and Asperger's Syndrome with psychotropic medications, particularly antipsychotics.

12

MY CHILD CAN'T FOCUS, IS EASILY DISTRACTED, AND CAN'T STAY STILL!

Volumes have been written on attention deficit disorder/attention deficit hyperactivity disorder (ADD/ADHD), and for a time it seemed to be the diagnosis du jour for any child who couldn't sit still or pay attention in class. We now know that ADD extends far beyond that simplistic definition, and that it can follow young people as they grow up. In fact, 50 percent to 75 percent of children with this disorder will go on to experience symptoms in adolescence and adulthood. Alarmingly, approximately half of all children with untreated ADD/ADHD go on to experience substance-abuse problems in late adolescence or early adulthood. In total, ADD/ADHD disorder affects 5 percent to 8 percent of all children in the United States.

The differences between ADD and ADHD can be attributed to symptom presentation. Initially, there was ADD—or mental distractibility—which many believed was more a behavioral problem than a biological one. Mental distractibility was and remains the core symptom of this disorder. As time passed, however, the addition of hyperactivity to the mix prompted the Diagnostic and Statistical Manual of Mental Disorders, Fourth Edition (DSM-IV TR) to outline three subtypes of ADHD:

Inattentive: The child can sit still, but has difficulty focusing.

Hyperactive/impulsive: The child can focus, but has difficulty sitting still, and tends to speak and act impulsively without considering the consequences of their actions, either for themselves or others.

Combined: The child has difficulty focusing and sitting still, and tends to act impulsively.

The core features of inattention are characterized by difficulty paying attention for sustained periods; appearing not to listen; losing needed items; being easily distracted; carelessness; forgetfulness; difficulty organizing activities; failure to follow through on tasks; and avoiding activities that require prolonged mental effort.

The core features of hyperactivity-impulsivity are characterized by fidgeting or squirming; leaving one's seat during class; restlessness, running and climbing excessively; talking too much; responding to questions before the question is stated; interrupting others; and experiencing difficulty waiting for one's turn.

ADD/ADHD is:

- Four to nine times more common in boys among children
- Observable in children as young as age four; usual onset is age 7 to 8
- Often misdiagnosed, due to its frequent co-existence with conditions such as bipolar disorder, anxiety, depression, mental retardation, borderline personality disorder, conduct disorder, oppositional defiant disorder, Tourette's syndrome and trauma experiences
- Accompanied by poor frustration tolerance, transitional difficulties, possible sleep disturbances and poor self-image.

ADHD ETIOLOGY

Though initial theories focused on ADHD as a disorder of hyperarousal, an amazingly different view of the disorder has emerged from rigorous clinical investigations. The current clinical thinking is that the etiology of ADHD is not hyperarousal, but instead is primarily weakened "new brain" or prefrontal cortex circuitry that regulates attention and behavior. We have also learned that there is a significant genetic component associated with the disorder. As a result, norepinephrine and dopamine pathways are adversely affected. Both these neurotransmitters play a key role in the therapeutic effects of stimulant medications. Other, though unproven, theories focus on vitamin deficiencies, food additives and food allergies. Some nutritional approaches lean toward low-gluten diets and the addition of omega-3 fatty acid supplements. We do know that ADHD does *not* develop from sugar consumption.

MEDICATION MANAGEMENT OF ADD/ADHD

There are three classes of medications with proven effectiveness in the treatment of ADHD: psychostimulants, some antidepressants, and alpha 2 adrenergic agonists.

Figure 12.1 Medications for ADD/ADHD

Brand Name	Generic Name
Adderall	dextroamphetamine/amphetamine
Adderall XR	dextroamphetamine/amphetamine
Catapres	clonidine
Concerta	methylphenidate
Daytrana	methylphenidate transdermal
Dexedrine	dextroamphetamine
Dexedrine Spansule	dextroamphetamine
Dextrostat	dextroamphetamine
Focalin	dexmethylphenidate
Focalin XR	dexmethylphenidate
Metadate CD	methylphenidate
Methylin	methylphenidate
Ritalin	methylphenidate
Ritalin LA, SR	methylphenidate
Strattera	atomoxetine
Tenex	guanfacine
Wellbutrin	bupropion
Wellbutrin SR, LA	bupropion

Psychostimulants

The treatment of ADHD with psychostimulants has involved a long but steady evolutionary process over the last five decades. All of the psychostimulants, regardless of their onset of action or duration of action, increase prefrontal cortex levels of norepinephrine and dopamine. As such, the attentional and behavioral deficits associated with ADHD generally improve.

The first stimulants employed were immediate-release preparations of Ritalin (methylphenidate), Dexedrine (dextroamphetamine) and then the mixed amphetamine salt Adderall. A typical dosing regimen with these medications was to administer them three times daily—usually at 8 a.m., noon and 4 p.m. The problem with the immediate-release preparations is that between doses, symptoms may return, resulting in an unstable clinical course. As such, a child's school performance would typically worsen until the next dose was administered. Also, a multiple daily dosing regimen is inconvenient, and this led to noncompliance.

With the above in mind, the standard of care for treating ADHD has shifted to once-daily medications. The model of the newer generation, long-acting methylphenidate drugs is Concerta (methylphenidate). Concerta was designed to provide 12 hours of symptom coverage, which it does by essentially replacing three doses of immediate-release methylphenidate administered four hours apart. This 12-hour symptom management recognizes the importance of covering the school day and after-school hours, including homework.

After Concerta came other methylphenidate preparations, such as Metadate CD and Ritalin LA. These were formulated to replace two doses of immediate-release methylphenidate given four hours apart. In other words, they provide symptom coverage throughout the school day, but not after school. Also, an extended release mixed amphetamine salts (MAS-XR), going by the trade name Adderall XR, has become available.

One of the newest psychostimulant agents, Daytrana (methylphenidate transdermal system), is a transdermal methylphenidate patch that is absorbed through the skin, thereby bypassing some metabolism through the liver. It is designed to be applied for nine hours, works for 12 hours, and is one of the longest-acting compounds available. It also offers flexibility, in that the duration of delivery can be customized. Once the patch is removed, activity still continues for another three hours or so. If children have a short day, they can remove the patch earlier; if they have a long day—including homework that extends into the evening hours—they can leave the patch on.

First available in 2007, Vyvanse (lisdexamfetamine dimesylate) is the newest entry in the oral psychostimulant arena. It is also a long-acting agent to control ADHD symptoms throughout the day, particularly in the areas of focus, following instructions, hyperactivity and impulsivity. It is rapidly absorbed from the gastrointestinal tract and converted to dextroamphetamine and the amino acid l-lysine, with 12-hour symptom coverage. In an open-label clinical study, Vyvanse (lisdexamfetamine dimesylate) provided overall improvement in 95 percent of children taking the drug for 12 months. Also, the therapeutic action of Vyvanse (lisdexamfetamine dimesylate) is not realized unless the drug is swallowed and subjected to gastrointestinal absorption. This means it may possess lower abuse potential via intranasal and intravenous routes of administration, or if smoked, when compared with other oral psychostimulants.

Long-term use of psychostimulants is generally well tolerated. Common side effects include insomnia (particularly at the beginning of treatment), dry mouth, decrease in appetite and weight loss, minor changes in heart rate and blood pressure, and rebound effect, in which symptoms can worsen as the medication effects wear off. Weight loss is transient; most young subjects catch up in weight or height throughout the developmental cycle. There is some evidence that stimulants suppress the secretion of growth hormone during the years in which these medications are typically administered. Clinicians can gradually introduce dose reductions as patients get older, and at ages 14 to 16 most children have a growth spike regardless of medication use. Psychostimulants are considered C-II controlled substances by the FDA.

Antidepressants

Wellbutrin (bupropion) and Wellbutrin SR/LA can be helpful in treating ADHD, because like the psychostimulants, they can enhance the actions of norepinephrine and dopamine in the prefrontal cortex. SSRIs, on the other hand, due to their singular effects on serotonin, are considered poor choices in managing ADHD. From an efficacy standpoint, clinical trials indicate a clear advantage of stimulant use over Wellbutrin (bupropion). However, Wellbutrin (bupropion), as an antidepressant, can treat co-occurring depression and is not a controlled substance.

Strattera (atomoxetine) is a norepinephrine specific reuptake inhibitor (NRI) antidepressant. As such, it carries the same "black box" warning as do all other antidepressants for possible risk of suicide when used by children and adolescents. It was marketed for adult ADD before gaining FDA approval for use in children. Strattera (atomoxetine) fails miserably in head-to-head clinical trials versus the psychostimulants in managing ADHD, and long-term safety data on Strattera for use in children is not well established. Strattera (atmoxetine) has been linked to liver damage, and the drug's labeling warns that severe liver damage may progress to liver failure and the possible need for a transplant in a small percentage of patients.

Alpha-2 agonists

Catapres (clonidine) and Tenex (guanfacine) are antihypertensives used to control high blood pressure. They are also used to treat some anxiety conditions and to control hyperactivity and aggression, irritability, tics and Tourette's syndrome. They can be combined with the psychostimulants discussed above. Tenex (guanfacine) acts directly on the prefrontal cortex to improve the so-called "executive functions," including organization, planning and foresight. Catapres (clonidine) was for a time used to treat psychostimulant-induced insomnia, but several clinical and media reports in 1995 brought attention to the death of four children who had been receiving methylphenidate and clonidine concomitantly. Cardiovascular toxicity was suspected. As it turned out, all of the deaths were associated with multiple variables that precluded attributing the cause of death to this drug combination. Since the mid-1990s, there have been no further reports of any serious ramifications associated with the methylphenidate/clonidine combination, likely due to its less frequent usage.

Side effects of the Alpha-2 agonists are mild and uncommon. They include dizziness from low blood pressure, headache, nausea, depression and changes in heart rhythm. Drowsiness is the most common side effect. This can be addressed by first reducing the dosage, then increasing it gradually, if needed.

DRUG HOLIDAYS

The issue of drug "holidays"—a short-term, deliberate discontinuation of ADHD medication—is also known as a structured treatment interruption. These "holidays" can take place over a weekend, a full week or an extended school vacation. There is no definitive conclusion as to the benefits or drawbacks to drug holidays. Some physicians maintain that because ADHD is a chronic disorder, suspending treatment is not in the patient's best interest. But for parents who are concerned about "overdrugging" their children, drug holidays can be a welcome relief, even if only a perceived one.

According to a 2005 report in *Medscape Psychiatry and Mental Health*, there are three purposes to a drug holiday:

- To demonstrate the clinical need for medication
- To temporarily remove side effects
- To satisfy the notions of caregivers that medicine should not be used if it can be avoided.

The most frequently cited study examined 40 children on drug holidays, and it found that weekend holidays from the psychostimulants (methylphenidate) reduced insomnia and appetite suppression without significantly increasing ADHD symptoms; the behaviors were reported by the parents. This extended to the Monday following the weekend, as reported by the teachers. However, anecdotal reports by some physicians indicate that patients can experience difficulty adjusting to re-dosing for one to three days after their drug holiday is completed.

DOSAGE RANGE CHART — MEDICATIONS FOR ADD/ADHD

BRAND NAME	GENERIC NAME	DAILY DOSAGE RANGE *
Adderall	dextroamphetamine/ amphetamine	5 mg – 40 mg
Adderall XR	dextroamphetamine/ amphetamine	10 mg – 30 mg
Catapres	clonidine	0.1 mg - 0.4 mg **
Concerta	methylphenidate	18 mg - 108 mg
Daytrana	methylphenidate	10 mg – 30 mg (transdermal)
Dexedrine	dextroamphetamine	5 mg – 40 mg
Focalin	dexmethylphenidate	5 mg – 40 mg
Focalin XR	dexmethylphenidate	10 mg – 40 mg
Metadate CD	methylphenidate	20 mg – 60 mg
Methylin	methylphenidate	10 mg – 60 mg
Ritalin	methylphenidate	5 mg – 50 mg
Ritalin LA	methylphenidate	20 mg – 40 mg
Strattera	atomoxetine	60 mg – 120 mg
Tenex	guanfacine	0.25 mg - 1.0 mg ***
Vyvanse	lisdexamfetamine	30 mg – 70 mg
Wellbutrin SR, LA	bupropion	150 mg – 300 mg

* Suggested adult dose

** Dosed 2 to 4 times daily

*** Dosed 2 to 3 times daily

Note: Dosage ranges may vary depending on source, and may also vary according to age.

13

THE ALTERNATIVE MEDICINE FRENZY

To read the volumes of ever-increasing information on this subject, the latest "natural" miracle cure is either on the horizon or already here. There are many claims to fame in that regard, but most of them fall by the wayside if and when they are subjected to scientific research. You have no doubt seen in your practice the increased use of "self-prescribed" alternative remedies, often utilized by patients regardless of whether these remedies were recommended by their health practitioners. For this reason, I am including these alternatives. My goal is to help you become aware of their uses, recommended dosages, side effects and possibly adverse actions.

Of the literally hundreds of herbals, supplements and vitamins that are touted as being effective, five have emerged with various levels of documented efficacy in the treatment of mental health disorders. This is by no means a complete list, and many experts disagree on the definitions of efficacy, but these are the ones that demonstrate credible evidence to back up their claims.

However, simply because they are not prescription drugs does not mean they don't have side effects, which, like those of any medication, can range from unpleasant to dangerous. It is therefore important for clinicians to know whether patients are taking any of the following, or any other alternative treatments for their conditions. Clinicians must then monitor for interactions and possible adverse effects.

Figure 13-1. Possible Side Effects of Alternative Remedies

St. John's Wort	• Restlessness, fatigue, dizziness and increased sensitivity to sunlight (photosensitivity). • May interact with oral contraceptives and reduce their effectiveness. • Potentially serious interactions with prescription antidepressants, resulting in rapid heartbeat, agitation, tremors and other symptoms of elevated serotonin levels in the brain (serotonin syndrome).
SAM-e	• Gastrointestinal symptoms (stomach upset, nausea, vomiting), insomnia, anxiety. • May interact with some prescription antidepressants, resulting in rapid heartbeat, agitation, tremors and other symptoms of elevated serotonin levels in the brain (serotonin syndrome). • Warning: SAMe should not be used in patients with bipolar disorder (manic-depressive illness).
Melatonin	• Gastrointestinal symptoms, drowsiness, depression, headache, lethargy, ovulation inhibition and suppression of male sex drive. • Risk of additional sedation if combined with alcohol. • May interfere with drugs such as Deltasone (prednisone).
Ginko Biloba	• Headache, dizziness, restlessness, racing heart and gastrointestinal symptoms. • Caution should be taken in patients with diabetes, hypoglycemia or other blood-sugar issues, as gingko can theoretically affect blood-sugar levels. Monitoring is recommended for patients taking other medications that affect blood sugar. • Can affect the outcome of electroconvulsive therapy (ECT).
Omega-3 Fatty Acids	• Increased risk of bruising. • May increase the risk of bleeding when combined with aspirin or other blood thinners.

St. John's Wort

This humble yellow wildflower, named after St. John the Baptist, became an "overnight sensation" in America after being used for thousands of years in Europe, and even by Native Americans, for a variety of ailments. It has risen to the top as probably one of the most effective herbal remedies in the treatment of mild depression. Once thought to mimic the actions of the monoamine oxidase inhibitors (MAOIs), recent findings indicate that it is more likely similar in action to the SSRIs, leading to its nickname of "nature's Prozac."

One area of similarity to the MAOIs, however, is the high incidence of drug/drug interactions that occur with St. John's Wort. For this reason, this herbal is almost always recommended to be taken alone. This minimizes, as much as possible, the significant and potentially problematic interactions with prescription medications or other herbals. Complicating matters further, St. John's Wort is not a single substance. Rather, it is a complex mix of at least 10 groups of active ingredients that involve antidepressant, anti-inflammatory, antibacterial, antiviral, sedative and diuretic properties.

One of the problems with determining drug interactions associated with St. John's Wort is that, as an herbal, it is not FDA-regulated. Because of its pharmacology, St. John's Wort should not be used in combination with prescription serotonin reuptake inhibitors. This combination can lead to serotonin syndrome with its symptoms of mania, hypomania, anxiety, agitation, rigidity and fever. Also, St. John's Wort should be avoided by pregnant women. Studies show that this herbal can reduce the anticoagulant effect of the blood thinner warfarin and can lower plasma concentrations of the cardiac medication digoxin. It is also known to decrease the efficacy of oral contraceptives. One side effect of St. John's Wort is photosensitivity, or an abnormal sensitivity to light, especially of the eyes.

St. John's Wort has been used extensively in Germany, where many of the most notable studies have taken place. Although this herbal has been successful in treating mild to moderate depression—enough to earn approval from Germany's Commission E—its effects on major depressive disorder are less promising. The usual adult dose is 900 mg per day, usually in divided doses of 300 mg each.

SAMe (S-adenosylmethionine)

SAMe is considered by many to be one of the best natural antidepressants in the treatment of mild to moderate depression. This made SAMe headline news when it first hit the U.S. market in 1999. SAMe (S-adenosylmethionine) is a substance found in the body that helps in the production of neurotransmitters and hormones aided by the amino acid methionine. Ordinarily, the brain manufactures all the SAMe it needs, but in depression, methionine synthesis is impaired.

SAMe has been the subject of more than 100 trials around the world. Some of these studies show that it effectively mimics the action of the selective serotonin reuptake inhibitors (SSRIs), which we have previously discussed as instrumental in the treatment of depression. In some recent studies, SAMe has performed as well as antidepressant drugs, including SSRIs. It is also used in the treatment of fibromyalgia, a chronic disorder characterized by widespread muscle pain accompanied by depression and anxiety. Although there is no standard dose, SAMe appears to be effective particularly in mild depression at doses of 400 mg per day.

In 2004 researchers from Harvard Medical School found that SAMe was beneficial in treatment-resistant depression by combining it with conventional antidepressants for those whose symptoms had not responded to the antidepressant alone. The results of this study showed a positive response to the therapy, with improved scores on the Hamilton Depression scale and Montgomery-Asberg Depression Rating scale, two instruments that measure the severity of depression.

A 1994 report of 13 clinical trials concluded that the efficacy of SAMe in treating depressive syndromes and disorders is superior to that of placebo and comparable to that of standard tricyclic antidepressants. These findings were confirmed in a 2002 report presented by the Agency for Healthcare Research and Quality.

Due to its high cost, SAMe has never really taken off as a treatment for depression in the United States. A one-month supply in its oral form can run as high as $60, putting SAMe in line, cost-wise, with some prescription antidepressants. Also, people with bipolar disorder should not take SAMe due to a number of reported cases whereby patients have experienced manic or hypomanic episodes.

Melatonin

Melatonin can be your best friend if you have difficulty getting to sleep. It is a hormone manufactured by the pineal gland in the brain from the amino acid tryptophan. Melatonin may be connected to letting our bodies know when it is time to fall sleep and wake up. Melatonin is synthesized and released during darkness, and natural levels are present in the blood prior to bedtime. In people older than 40 years, the pineal gland has likely slowed down its production of melatonin, and by age 50, virtually everyone has a melatonin deficiency. Melatonin is primarily used in cases of insomnia, and it may also be taken to prevent jet lag associated with long air travel.

According to the NIMH, multiple human studies have measured the effects of melatonin supplements on sleep in healthy individuals. Although most of the trials have been small and brief, the weight of scientific evidence suggests that melatonin decreases the time needed to fall asleep, increases feelings of sleepiness, and increases the duration of sleep. For use in adults in the treatment of insomnia, a dose of 0.3 mg at bedtime, preferably about one hour before retiring, is generally sufficient.

There is also some suggestion that melatonin can improve sleep disorders associated with Alzheimer's disease, specifically night time agitation and poor sleep quality, but further research is needed. In addition, a limited study of patients with bipolar disorder attempted to determine if insomnia or irregular sleep patterns could be improved with melatonin, but no clear benefits were reported.

Another area of melatonin research by the NIMH addressed sleep disturbances in children with neuro-psychiatric disorders, such as mental retardation, autism and psychiatric disorders. These studies demonstrated a reduced time to fall asleep, an increased duration of sleep, and credible scientific evidence for its use.

Areas in which further study is required include ADHD in children, benzodiazepine tapering, sleep disturbances associated with depression and schizophrenia, and the use of melatonin to treat tardive dyskinesia.

Gingko Biloba

Gingko biloba is one of the top-selling herbal supplements in the United States. With an aging population and the attendant scare of Alzheimer's disease, people have been buying gingko for years in the hopes that it will improve their memory. Since the 1950s, more than 400 papers on ginkgo—the majority from German investigators—have appeared in the medical literature.

Unfortunately, gingko biloba has failed in trials with regard to memory improvement. But there is good news: The scientific literature suggests that gingko benefits those with early-stage Alzheimer's and multi-infarct dementia (memory loss due to disruption in blood flow to the brain). In fact, gingko may actually be as helpful as the Alzheimer's drug Aricept (donepezil), in that it appears to slow cognitive decline in dementia.

A report published by the Oregon Health Sciences University and the Portland Veterans Affairs Medical Center synthesized the data from four major controlled studies. They show that there was a "small but significant effect" from treatment of three to six months with 120 mg to 140 mg of gingko biloba extract on objective measures of cognitive function in Alzheimer's.

Gingko appears to work most effectively in disorders having to do with circulatory problems, both neurodegenerative and vascular diseases that involve poor blood flow to the brain due to narrowed blood vessels or strokes. It is a potent antioxidant (that is, it protects cells from damage), and its main agents are thought to be unique chemicals called ginkgolides. It is also an anticoagulant—meaning it reduces the stickiness of blood platelets and the formation of blood clots—and has anti-inflammatory properties.

Traditional Chinese medicine (TCM) practitioners have for thousands of years used ginko derived from a tree native to China and Japan. Extracts of this herbal have been used to treat a variety of disorders. So far it is showing its best results—in addition to slowing cognitive decline—in the management of intermittent claudication, which is leg pain due to insufficient circulation; and cerebral insufficiency, a syndrome secondary to atherosclerotic disease characterized by confusion, impaired concentration, dizziness, anxiety and depression. Gingko may also help improve blood flow to the heart, provide an immune system boost, and help to reduce free radical damage. Again, its main benefit appears to come from its stellar properties as a circulatory stimulant.

Omega-3 fatty acids

"Fat" has become a bad word in our society, but the fact is that a particular type of fat is so essential, our body's cells can literally collapse without it. Fish oil—with its singular component omega-3 fatty acids and in conjunction with other types of fat in the membranes that surround the cells—literally control cell behavior. Reportedly, even a tiny imbalance can create crippling dysfunction throughout the body.

Fish oils are made up of EPA (eicosapentaenoic acid), critical in heart function, and DHA (docosahexaenoic acid), critical in brain function. These oils are found in fatty fish like salmon, mackerel, tuna and sardines, as well as in supplements in gelcap form. Both DHA and EPA affect calcium, sodium, and potassium ion channels that regulate cellular electrical activity in the heart and the brain.

Omega-3 fatty acids have been well established with regard to improving nerve conduction, and they are well on their way to being recognized as effective in the management of depression by regulating neurotransmitters like serotonin and dopamine. Studies have shown a correlation between low levels of omega-3s and depression, and trials using omega-3s are showing promising results in the use of this supplement as a treatment for depression.

For example, a 2002 study was conducted in England with 60 men and women suffering from treatment-resistant depression (depression that did not respond to conventional medications). Those taking 1 gram of EPA per day showed significantly greater improvement on depression-measuring scales than did the placebo group.

In another study, this one of 30 patients with bipolar disorder led by a researcher at Harvard Medical School, the group that took 9.6 grams of omega-3 acids daily (EPA and DHA) showed "significant symptom reduction and a better outcome when compared to placebo [olive oil alone]." The conclusion was that the omega-3 fatty acids were well tolerated and improved the short-term course of illness.

The typical American diet is high in omega-6 compared to omega-3, prompting experts to recommend at least three servings of fish a week to maintain a balance between omega-3 and omega-6 fatty acids. While omega-6 oils (corn, soybean) can generate an inflammatory reaction, omega-3 oils found in cold-water fish work by subduing inflammation, which is why they are often used to alleviate the symptoms of rheumatoid arthritis, cancer, and Crohn's disease. The human body can also manufacture omega-3s from walnuts and flaxseed.

According to some experts, the rising rates of depression in this country could be partially explained by the rising ratios in omega-6 fatty acids. Although there is no conclusive proof of this theory, some practitioners are recommending "mood enhancing diets" for their patients that include eating more fish and adding an omega-3 supplement. In Japan and other countries where fish consumption is high, the rates of depression and heart disease are comparatively low.

14

WHAT'S NEXT, AND WHAT CAN WE EXPECT?

What will be the next big thing in psychopharmacology? Research in this field is constantly ongoing, with new discoveries and possibilities emerging all the time. Approximately 8 percent of people take psychotropic medication, and psychiatric drug use in children has tripled in just 10 years. Not surprisingly, medication designed to affect brain chemistry that regulates mood represents the hottest segment of the pharmaceutical market.

According to industry analysts, drugs for depression will enjoy a growing demand. As of 2008, 44 medications currently under development focus on depression. In fact, the World Health Organization (WHO) predicts that depression will become the leading contributor to the global burden of disease by the year 2020. Since the 1980s, drug company investment in central nervous system research has been unprecedented, with drugs for anxiety and depression leading the pack. Prozac was the superstar of the 1990s. And in this book, we have examined depression and anxiety associated with the exacerbation of the fight-or-flight syndrome, and the antidepressants and anti-anxiety agents used to manage it. What do we see coming down the drug pipeline in the coming years?

I believe the wave of the future in managing anxiety and depression will likely focus on the association between stress hormone secretion and the wide range of resulting physiological responses. Two of these stress hormones are corticotropin-releasing factor (CRF)—also known as corticotropin-releasing hormone (CRH)—and Substance P. Both of these coordinate responses to stress. They are released through the hypothalamus; excessive secretion can lead to possibly debilitating states of anxiety and subsequent depression. For example, excessive levels of CRH have been found in the cerebrospinal fluid of suicide victims. As of this writing, there are no medications on the U.S. market that address this issue, although there is at least one ongoing study on the CRH-1 antagonist pexacerfont in outpatients diagnosed with generalized anxiety disorder (GAD).

Similarly, increasing attention is being paid to the stress hormone cortisol. Cortisol overproduction has been linked to changes in blood sugar levels and blood pressure, fat redistribution (especially accumulation around the middle), immune system compromise (an infection waiting to happen), and the shrinkage of brain cells.

Substance P has been associated with regulating anxiety, stress and mood disorder. It functions as a neurotransmitter, especially with regard to pain impulses from peripheral receptors to the central nervous system. The higher the level of Substance P, the more efficient the pain transmission system. Substance P was first discovered in the 1930s, and there is today an enormous amount of research in this area. Researchers have studied its effect on the peripheral nerves, the brain and the spinal cord. Researchers are also looking at the influence of serotonin, specifically how it controls the levels of Substance P.

Also, evidence indicates that testosterone may play a role in male depression, particularly in mid- to late-life. Men with the lowest levels of testosterone are more than three times more likely to suffer from depression than those with the highest levels, according to the research. To help this group, testosterone supplement products are being developed. A study at McLean Hospital in Massachusetts tested 54 men whose symptoms of depression were not alleviated by antidepressants. It found that 43 percent of them had low testosterone levels. The group that received a testosterone gel for eight weeks exhibited significant improvement in mood, sleep, appetite and libido.

While it's impossible to predict which new drugs will survive development, research and testing, and eventually make it all the way to market, teams of well educated and highly experienced professionals worldwide will continue to seek the next breakthroughs in psychopharmacology.

In closing, as I look back at my 30-plus-year career of studying, teaching and researching this field, I am delighted by how far we have come. Yet for those plagued by the woes of mental illness, medication doesn't make them whole again. Instead, it serves as but one component of an integrated plan of care geared toward maximizing positive clinical outcomes. I look forward to what comes next as science continues to unravel the complex mysteries of the human brain.

— Joseph Wegmann, R.Ph., L.C.S.W.

APPENDIX I

MAKING A MEDICATION REFERRAL

Throughout the many years I have practiced psychotherapy, the area where I still consistently encounter the most client resistance is the use of medication to augment therapy treatment. Years ago, when I was a novice psychotherapist, I believed that clients would go along willingly with the suggestions and recommendations put forth by their trusted therapist. How wrong I was! Thankfully, what I figured out in relatively short order was this: When it comes to medication, clients will make their own choices, on their own terms, and in their own time.

But even when faced with client ambivalence, I consider it an obligation to voice my views on the most viable, literature-grounded alternatives available. I ensure that my patients have as much information as I can provide, so that they can make informed choices about their future treatment.

With this in mind, here are a select few of the markers to take into account when considering a referral for psychotropic medication with a patient:

- The patient is not responding favorably to psychotherapy, despite an adequate trial period. For me, this is number one.
- The patient has a complicated medical history and is taking multiple medications. Never underestimate the negative influence that certain medical disorders and some prescription medications can have on client improvement.

- The patient hasn't had a thorough physical examination in years. There may be an undiagnosed medical condition that is impinging upon what the client sought treatment for in the first place.
- The patient initially presents with prominent mood and behavior instabilities, or mood and behavior become more markedly labile as psychotherapy continues.
- There is an active and identifiable presence of psychotic features exhibited by the patient. This is evidence of a biologically based disorder, for which pharmacological intervention is the mainstay of treatment, with psychotherapy as an adjunct to care.
- A prolonged personal history or significant family history of mental disturbance.

Substance abuse may be associated with the patient that repeatedly experiences relapses after some improvement. Also, many of the disorders discussed in this book are highly heritable. Genetic predispositions often are associated with neurochemical deficits in the brain that can have an adverse influence on sustained symptom improvement unless pharmacotherapy is considered.

APPENDIX II

FREQUENTLY ASKED QUESTIONS

Q. Why do so many antidepressants seem to cause sexual dysfunction?

A. In addition to its antidepressant effects, serotonin is a rather powerful vasoconstrictor. It can restrict blood flow to sexual organs and negatively impact sexual performance, libido and the ability to reach orgasm.

Q. What is the safety profile of the SSRIs?

A. From a "potential for overdose" perspective, they are actually incredibly safe. Death by SSRI overdose, according to some published reports, occurs in only about two out of every 1 million individuals using them.

Q. Is Prozac's long half-life a drawback to its action?

A. Yes and no. Prozac's long half-life can be an advantage to the individual prone to forget doses, but a disadvantage to those taking additional medications (and not only psychotropics). For example, Prozac has been reported to increase the effect of the cyclic antidepressant Norpramin (desipramine) by 400-fold in some subjects! It can also increase the effects of some benzodiazepines.

Q. How does Cymbalta differ from Effexor?

A. Both are classified as serotonin/norepinephrine reuptake inhibitors (SNRIs). However, Cymbalta is a more potent reuptake inhibitor of these neurotransmitters, and it has garnered FDA approval for the management of diabetic neuropathic pain (diabetic neuropathy).

Q. Is the diagnosis of pediatric bipolar disorder on the rise?

A. Definitely yes. According to a commentary in the December 2007 *Harvard Mental Health Letter*, office visits by children diagnosed with bipolar disorder multiplied 40-fold from 1994 to 2003. The number of office visits per 100,000 children rose from 25 to 1,003 in the same period.

Q. For treating depression, are the older cyclic antidepressants as effective as the newer SSRIs, SNRIs and atypicals?

A. In my estimation, yes. Most of the cyclics are dual-action—that is, they assist at increasing the availability of norepinephrine and serotonin to the "emotional brain." And they were doing so years before the advent of the more-widely prescribed SSRIs and SNRIs.

Q. Why is Topamax linked to weight loss in some subjects?

A. Topamax is an interesting drug, to say the least. Reports indicate that it was originally developed as an anti-diabetic agent, but that didn't come to pass. There is some evidence that Topamax improves insulin sensitivity, and with better management of glucose, weight loss can occur.

Q. Are recent reports regarding sleepwalking, "sleep eating" and "sleep driving" with Ambien use true?

A. Yes, but the number of *reported* cases is still small. Nevertheless, some people using Ambien report objective evidence of having engaged in these behaviors with no recollection the next day of having done so. In rare instances, Ambien may disrupt the sleep/wake cycle in some users.

Q. Are Risperdal and Invega similar?

A. Invega is actually an active metabolite of Risperdal, thus their antipsychotic actions are similar. However, Invega has an extended-release delivery system that allows for once-daily dosing, unlike Risperdal.

Q. Is Lamictal safe for use during pregnancy?

A. Unlike its predecessors Tegretol and Depakote, Lamictal does not seem to increase the risk of major birth malformations if used during pregnancy. Still, it is advisable that it not be taken during the first trimester of pregnancy.

Q. Is Wellbutrin effective in treating ADHD?

A. Yes, although primarily as an augmenting agent to the methylphenidate and dextroamphetamine type psychostimulants, which are the mainstay of treating ADHD. Wellbutrin is also effective in treating ADHD and co-morbid depression.

Q. In treating ADHD, are there any advantages to using Vyvanse over Adderall XR?

A. Both ostensibly provide 10- to 12-hour symptom coverage. But Vyvanse needs to be completely absorbed via the gastrointestinal tract before converting to d-amphetamine, thus minimizing the risk that this compound can be abused through the intranasal and intravenous route, or even smoked.

Q. Is Deplin an antidepressant?

A. No, Deplin is actually a methylfolate preparation. Depressed patients consistently have lower serum folate concentrations. Deplin helps normalize amounts of the neurotransmitters norpinephrine, serotonin and dopamine, thus enabling antidepressants to be more effective.

Q. In relationship to OCD, what is "PANDAS?"

A. PANDAS is the acronym for Pediatric Autoimmune Neuropsychiatric Disorders Associated with Streptococcal infections. This is actually a subtype of pediatric OCD, triggered by strep throat, in which the body's own immune cells attack the basal ganglia within the brain rather than the strep. PANDAS OCD is usually consistent with the *sudden onset* of OCD symptoms.

Q. Why do most psychotropic medications seem to cause weight gain?

A. Many psychiatric medications slow the metabolism of carbohydrate and fat. Also, some psychotropics, such as the antipsychotics Clozaril and Zyprexa, interfere with satiety. People taking these medications often continue to eat and eat—particularly sugars — without feeling full.

APPENDIX III

MEDICATION NONCOMPLIANCE

Think of this as the "other" drug problem. Sometimes, even with the most effective drugs, careful monitoring and strict adherence to prescribed guidelines, some patients still don't improve. There may be many reasons for this, some of which can be addressed by more effective communication with prescribers, switching medications or combining drugs with other therapies.

But here's a certainty: Medication that routinely remains in the vial or bottle won't help anyone.

Millions of people fail to take their medication correctly. This is called medication non-compliance, and it is a serious problem. Worse, some quit taking their medication altogether, without giving any consideration to discussing their intentions with their prescribers or other health care providers.

Consider these findings on medication non-compliance from the nonprofit National Council on Patient Information and Education:

- Only 50 percent of patients with heart disease, asthma or hypertension follow prescribing directions.
- Adherence to prescribing guidelines is a problem for all age groups, and it is not just an issue of poverty or poor education. Even the wealthy and most educated among us skip their medication.

- Consequences don't necessarily enhance compliance. Only 58 percent of glaucoma patients already blind in one eye were protecting their other eye.
- Doctors mess up, too! One study indicated physicians adhered to their own prescriptions less than 80 percent of the time.
- Noncompliance can run an extra $2,000 per year for each patient in additional doctor visits alone.

Some might say that the high cost of prescription drugs contributes to the problem, but medication noncompliance goes far beyond prescription affordability. So why does it seem to be so doggone hard to take a pill correctly as prescribed?

Because of hurried visits at the doctor's office, many people leave with new prescriptions without having asked a single question about the prescribed drug. Others purchase their medications, but misunderstand or even ignore label directions and how much they are supposed to take. Anybody can forget a dose of course. But many, after they begin feeling better, toss out the remainder of the prescription. Also, there is no doubt that the fear of side effects is a principal reason.

Another factor driving noncompliance, in my estimation, is intimidation. Nowadays, there is as much information stapled to the prescription bag as one might find in the Physicians Desk Reference. This results in information overkill, turning an ordinarily compliant patient into a noncompliant one out of fear of or confusion about what they've just read.

In addition, some prescription drug bottles and vials are covered with so many brightly colored warning stickers they resemble a tiny Christmas tree. Then there's the label, with wording that is often open to interpretation, and in tiny print that might require a floodlight to read. Literacy aside, it is amazing how many people attempt to take medications without the obvious benefits of proper lighting.

So with the above in mind, help is on the way. First, ask clients about recent or upcoming physician visits. Then offer them a checklist that will help keep them medication-compliant:

- Before leaving your doctor's office with a new prescription, ask detailed questions. For example: How and when do I take this drug? Are there any foods, beverages or other medications I should avoid while taking this drug? What is this drug supposed to do, and how can I tell if it is working? What side effects might I have, and what should I do about them? When do I discontinue this medication?
- At each doctor visit, bring a complete list of all prescription and non-prescription medications, including the names of any vitamins and supplements. This way, the physician can screen for possible interactions.
- If you can't read or understand the medication information sheet, ask a pharmacist for help. They can simplify complex and confusing directions.
- If forgetfulness is an issue, consider compartmentalized pillboxes or even a high-tech "talking" model that sounds an alarm when a dose is missed.

APPENDIX IV

MASTER DRUG CHART

Brand Name	Generic Name
Abilify	aripiprazole
Adapin	doxepin
Adderall	dextroamphetamine/amphetamine
Adderall XR	dextroamphetamine/amphetamine
Ambien	zolpidem
Anafranil	clomipramine
Asendin	amoxapine
Atarax	hydroxyzine
Ativan	lorazepam
Aventyl	nortriptyline
BuSpar	buspirone
Catapres	clonidine
Celexa	citalopram
Centrax	prazepam
Clozaril	clozapine
Concerta	methylphenidate
Cymbalta	duloxetine
Daytrana (transdermal)	methylphenidate
Depakote	divalproex
Desyrel	trazodone
Dexedrine	dextroamphetamine
Dexedrine Spansule	dextroamphetamine
Dextrostat	dextroamphetamine

Effexor	venlafaxine
Effexor SR	venlafaxine SR
Elavil	amitriptyline
Emsam (transdermal)	selegiline
Eskalith	lithium carbonate
Focalin	dexmethylphenidate
Focalin XR	dexmethylphenidate XR
Gabitril	tiagabine
Geodon	ziprasidone
Haldol	haloperidol
Inderal	propranolol
Invega	paliperidone
Klonopin	clonazepam
Lamictal	lamotrigine
Lexapro	escitalopram
Librium	chlordiazepoxide
Loxitane	loxapine
Ludiomil	maprotiline
Lunesta	eszopiclone
Luvox	fluvoxamine
Mellaril	thioridazine
Metadate CD	methylphenidate
Methylin	methylphenidate
Moban	molindone
Nardil	phenelzine
Navane	thiothixene
Neurontin	gabapentin
Norpramin	desipramine
Orap	pimozide
Pamelor	nortriptyline
Parnate	tranylcypromine
Paxil	paroxetine
Prolixin	fluphenazine
Prozac	fluoxetine
Remeron	mirtazapine
Risperdal	risperidone
Ritalin	methylphenidate

Ritalin LA	methylphenidate LA
Ritalin SR	methylphenidate SR
Rozerem	ramelteon
Sarafem	fluoxetine
Serax	oxazepam
Serentil	mesoridazine
Seroquel	quetiapine
Sinequan	doxepin
Sonata	zaleplon
Stelazine	trifluoperazine
Strattera	atomoxetine
Surmontil	trimipramine
Symbyax	olanzapine/fluoxetine
Tegretol	carbamazepine
Tenex	guanfacine
Tenormin	atenolol
Thorazine	chlorpromazine
Tofranil	imipramine
Topamax	topiramate
Tranxene	clorazepate
Trilafon	perphenazine
Trileptal	oxcarbazepine
Valium	diazepam
Vistaril	hydroxyzine
Vivactil	protriptyline
Vyvanse	lisdexamfetamine
Wellbutrin	bupropion
Wellbutrin LA	bupropion LA
Wellbutrin SR	bupropion SR
Xanax	alprazolam
Zoloft	sertraline
Zyprexa	olanzapine

RESOURCES

_____. 2002. Antidepressants for the Heart. *Harvard Mental Health Letter.* 18:9.

_____. 2002. Disaster and Trauma. *Harvard Mental Health Letter.* 18:7.

Agency for Healthcare Research and Quality. 2002. S-adenosyl-L-methionine for treatment of depression, osteoarthritis, and liver disease. Summary Report, AHRQ Publication No. 02-E033. Rockville, MD: Agency for Healthcare Research and Quality, ahrq.gov.

Ainsworth, P. 2000. *Understanding Depression.* Jackson, MS: University Press of Mississippi.

Akiskal, H. S. 1996. The prevalent clinical spectrum of bipolar disorders: beyond DSM-IV. *Journal of Clinical Psychopharmacology.* 16:(suppl) 4s–14s.

American Academy of Neurology. 2008. "Does Gingko Biloba Affect Memory?" sciencedaily.com.

American Psychiatric Association, *The DSM IV,* American Psychiatric Association, 1994.

Anderson, P. 2008. "Low Testosterone Levels Linked with Higher Risk of Depression." *Medscape Medical News,* medscape.com.

Appleton, W. 2000. *Prozac and the New Antidepressants.* New York: Penguin Putnam, Inc.

Arato, M., C.M. Banki, G. Bissette, C.B. Nemeroff. 1989. Elevated CSF CRF in suicide victims. *Biological Psychiatry* 25(3):355–359.

Arnstein, Amy F.T. 2007. "Alpha-2 agonists in the treatment of ADHD." *Medscape Psychiatry & Mental Health,* medscape.com.

Beaubrun, G., and G. E. Gary. 2000. A review of herbal medicines for psychiatric disorders. *Psychiatric Services* 51(9):1130–1134.

Bender, K. J., ed. 1993. Narcotic agents for alcoholism. *Psychotropics.* 13:6–8.

Benet, L. Z., J. R. Mitchell, and L. B. Sherner. 1990a. General Principles. In *Goodman & Gilman's: The Pharmacological Basis of Therapeutics.* A. G. Gilman, T. W. Rall, A. S. Nies, and P. Taylor, eds. New York: Pergamon Press.

Bentley, K., and Walsh, J. 2001. *The Social Worker and Pyschotropic Medication*. 2nd Edition. New York: The Free Press.

Brown, S. A. and M. A. Schuckit. 1988. Changes in depression among abstinent alcoholics. *Journal of the Study of Alcoholism.* 49:412–417.

Charney, D.S., Nemeroff, C.B., Braun, S. 2004. *The Peace of Mind Prescription: An Authoritative Guide to Finding the Most Effective Treatment for Anxiety and Depression*. Boston: Houghton Mifflin.

Cowley, G., et al. 1990. A breakthrough drug for depression. *Newsweek*, March 26.

Davis, J. M. et al. A meta-analysis of the efficacy of second generation antipsychotics. *Archives of General Psychiatry 2003*. June; 60:553–64.

Diamond, R. 2002. *Instant Psychopharmacology*. 2nd Edition. New York: W. W. Norton and Company.

Dubovsky, s. 2003. Fluoxetine safety during pregnancy and lactation. *Journal Watch Psychiatry*. 9:7.

Einarson, A. 2005. "The safety of psychotropic drug use during pregnancy: a review." *Medscape General Medicine. 7(4),* medscape.com.

Empfield, M., Bakalar, N. 2001. *Understanding Teenage Depression: A Guide to Diagnosis, Treatment, and Management*. New York: H. Holt.

Fowler, M. 2001. *Maybe You Know My Teen: A Parent's Guide to Helping Your Adolescent with Attention Deficit Hyperactivity Disorder*. New York: Broadway Books.

Geller, B. 2003. Serotonergic symptoms in SSRI exposed infants. *Journal Watch Psychiatry.* 9:10.

Geller, B. Antidepressants during pregnancy: benefits for children. *Journal Watch Psychiatry.* 9:1.

Ghaemi, S. N. 2000. New treatments for bipolar disorder: the role of atypical neuroleptic agents. *Journal of Clinical Psychopharmacology.* 61: (suppl)33–42.

Gitlin, M. 1996. Neurology/Psychiatry Update. *Pharmacist's Letter.* 18:3.

Gitlin, M.J. 1996. *The Psychotherapist's Guide to Psychopharmacology*. 2nd Edition. New York: Free Press.

Glazener, F. S. 1992. Adverse drug reactions. In *Melmon and Morrelli's Clinical Pharmacology: Basic Principles in Theraputics*. 3rd Edition. D. W. Nierenberg, ed. New York: McGraw-Hill.

Harvard Medical School. 2008. A SAD Story: Seasonal Affective Disorder. *Harvard Health Letter*.

Harvard University. 2003. Study Suggests Depressed Men May Benefit from Testosterone Replacement Therapy. hms.Harvard.edu/news/

Helgoe, L.A., Wilhelm, L.R., Kommor, M.J. 2005. *The Anxiety Answer Book*. Naperville, IL: Sourcebooks.

Hoffman, R.E., et al. 2000. Transcranial magnetic stimulation and auditory hallucinations in schizophrenia. *Lancet.* 355:1073–1075.

Jellin, J. 2002. Neurology/Psychiatry Update. *Pharmacists Letter.* 18:10.

Jellin, J. 2002. Pediatrics Update. *Pharmacists Letter.* 18:8.

Jellin, J. 2002. Psychotropic Medication Update. *The Brown University Child and Adolescent Psychopharmacology Update.* 4:10, 5:2.

Johnson, B. A. et al. 2003. Oral topiramate for treatment of alcohol dependence. *Lancet.* May 17; 261:1677-85

Kraepelin, E. 1921. *Textbook of Psychiatry*, 7th Edition. (abstracted). Translated by Diefendorf. London: MacMillan 1907.

Kramer, P.D. 1997. *Listening to Prozac: The Landmark Book About Antidepressant and the Remaking of the Self.* Revised Edition. New York: Penguin.

LaPlante, B.J. 2007. "Atypical antipsychotics and bipolar disorder." *Medscape Psychiatry & Mental Health,* medscape.com.

Manos, M. J. 2005. "Opinions on drug holidays in pediatric ADHD." *Medscape Psychiatry & Mental Health.* 10(2), medscape.com.

Martin, A., Scahill, L., Charney, D., and Leckman, J. 2003. *Pediatric Psychopharmacology, Principles and Practice.* New York, NY: Oxford University Press, Inc.

Mayo Foundation for Medical Education and Research. 2006. "Electroconvulsive Therapy (ECT): Treating Severe Depression and Mental Illness," mayoclinic.com.

Miller, R., Mason, S.E., eds. 2002. *Diagnosis: Schizophrenia: A Comprehensive Resource for Patients, Families, and Helping Professionals.* New York: Columbia University Press.

Mischoulon, D., et al. 1999. Strategies for augmentation of SSRI treatment: a survey of an academic psychopharmacology practice. *Harvard Review of Psychiatry.* 6:322–326.

National Institute of Mental Health, National Institutes of Health. 2007. Meeting Summary: "Childhood and Adolescent Onset Schizophrenia: Research Challenges and Opportunities," nimh.nih.gov.

Neziroglu, F., Yaryura-Tobias, J.A. 1997. *Over and Over Again: Understanding Obsessive-Compulsive Disorder*. San Francisco: Jossey-Bass.

Nidhino, S. E., E. Mignot, and W. C. Dement. 1998. Sedative-hypnotics. In *Textbook of Psychopharmacology*. 2nd Edition. A. F. Schatzberg and C. B. Nemeroff, eds. 487-502.

Osborn, I. 1998. *Tormenting Thoughts and Secret Rituals: The Hidden Epidemic of Obsessive-Compulsive Disorder*. New York: Pantheon Books.

Page, D. 2006. UCLA Develops Unique Nerve-stimulation Epilepsy Treatment, http://newsroom.ucla.edu.

Papolos, D., Papolos, J. 1999. *The Bipolar Child*. New York: Broadway Books.

PDR staff/editors. 2008. *Physicians' Desk Reference*. New York: Thomson Healthcare.

Peet, M., D.F. Horribin. 2002 A dose-ranging study of the effects of ethyl-eicosapentaenoate in patients with ongoing depression despite apparently adequate treatment with standard drugs. *Archives of General Psychiatry*, 59:913–919.

Perry, P. el al. 2002.Testosterone therapy in late-life major depression in males. *Journal of Clinical Psychiatry*. Dec. 63:12 1096–1101.

Pollock, V. E. 1992. Meta-analysis of subjective sensitivity to alcohol in sons of alcoholics. *American Journal of Psychiatry*. 149:1534–1538.

Porter, R. 2002. *Madness: A Brief History*. Oxford, NY: Oxford University Press.

Preston, J., O'Neal, M., and Talaga, M. 2002. *Handbook of Clinical Psychopharmacology for Therapists.* 3rd Edition. Oakland, CA: New Harbinger.

Rosen, L.E., Amador, X.F. 1996. *When Someone You Love is Depressed: How to Help Your Loved One without Losing Yourself.* New York: Free Press.

Roy-Byrne, P. 2003. Antidepressant effects of SAMe, Redux. *Journal Watch Psychiatry*. 9:1.

Roy-Byrne, P. 2003. The new ADHD drug atomoxetine: its mechanism for action. *Journal Watch Psychiatry*. 9:1.

Scherk, H., F.G. Pajonk, S. Leucht. 2007. Second-generation antipsychotic agents in the treatment of acute mania: a systematic review and meta-analysis of randomized controlled trials. *Archives of General Psychiatry*. 64(4):442–455.

Schildkraut, J. J. 1970. *Neuropsychopharmacology and the Affective Disorders* (New England Journal of Medicine Medical Progress Series). New York: Little, Brown.

Stahl, S. 1999. *Psychopharmacology of Antipsychotics*. London: Martin Dunitz.

Surman, C.B.H., R. Weisler. 2006. The state of the art treatment for pediatric and adolescent ADHD, medscape.com.

Terr, L. C. 1991. Childhood traumas: an outline and overview. *American Journal of Psychiatry*. 148:10–20.

Thase, M.E., R.H. Howland. 1995. Biological processes in depression: an updated review and integration. In *Handbook of Depression*. E. E. Beckham and W. R. Leber, eds. New York: Guilford Press.

Torrey, E.F. 2001. *Surviving Schizophrenia: A Manual for Families, Consumers, and Providers*. 4th Edition. New York: Quill.

Tucker, G. 2003 Antidepressants still don't seem to make a difference in bipolar depression. *Journal Watch Psychiatry*. 9:2.

Tucker, G. 2003. SSRIs during pregnancy: another view. *Journal Watch Psychiatry*. 9:7.

U.S. Food and Drug Administration. "Antidepressant Use in Children, Adolescents, and Adults," fda.gov.

White, R.F. 2006. "Pharmacologic advances in the treatment of ADHD in adults: an expert interview with Richard H. Weisler, MD." *Medscape Psychiatry & Mental Health* 11(1), medscape.com.

White, R.F. 2006. "Quality of life and treatment outcomes with once-daily medications for ADHD: an expert interview with Joseph Biederman, MD." *Medscape Psychiatry & Mental Health.* 11(1), medscape.com.

Wooten, J., J. Galavis. 2005. "Polypharmacy: Keeping the Elderly Safe," rnweb.com.

Zetin, M., and Tate, D. 1999. *The Psychopharmacology Sourcebook.* Lincolnwood, IL: Lowell House.

WEB SITES

Agency for Healthcare Research & Quality	ahrq.gov
American Academy of Child and Adolescent Psychiatry	aacap.org
American Psychiatric Association	psych.org
National Council on Patient Information and Education	talkaboutrx.org
National Institute of Mental Health, National Institutes of Health	nimh.nih.gov
National Mental Health Information Center, Substance Abuse and Mental Health Services (SAMHSA), U.S. Department of Health and Human Services	mentalhealth.samhsa.gov
U.S. Food and Drug Administration	fda.gov
World Health Organization	who.int

INDEX

O

P

Q

R